er Mark

Cairn

Wesserd

Old Barn

Quarry

Quiches

C G
Lookout

Links

Greenhow

Wheelers Hole

High Water Mark

Lower
Kennedy

Black
Forest

Main

Sandsloes

Straight Leaning

Chare Ends

Gat

Poles

St Coombs
Farm

Crooke

Bug Hall

Great
Close

The Basin

(Old Jetty)

Seaburn House

North Goat

Coffee
Chambers
BUS

P O
ROW

The Dyke
Hud

Easter Flue

Selby

Seasalt

St Cuthberts
Isle

Height

High Hude

Sand Flat

Low Water Mark

THE HARBOUR
4

Sandeel Beds

Long Bat

Low

South

Blac
La
Scar

Her
Stoo

Oyster Scap

Seabu
Scar

Quite
Point

The

Lindisfarne
Landscapes

Lindisfarne Landscapes

Sheila Mackay

SAINT ANDREW PRESS
1996

Published by
SAINT ANDREW PRESS
121 George Street, Edinburgh EH2 4YN

Copyright © Sheila Mackay 1996

ISBN 0 7152 0713 X

British Library Cataloguing in Publication Data
A catalogue record for this book
is available from the British Library

ISBN 071520713X

Cover painting and text illustrations
by Geoff MacEwan.
Cover design and original design format
by Mark Blackadder.
Typeset in 11/13 pt Garamond.
Printed and bound by Athenaeum Press Ltd.,
Gateshead, Tyne & Wear

CONTENTS

PREFACE

by Sheila Mackay

LINDISFARNE'S landscapes and history run in the very veins of its islanders. From them I learned what I know of its tides, winds, birds and wild flowers and glimpsed the rewards and the sacrifices of island life. During six treasured years as a part-time islander, I began the slow process of shedding my city guises in favour of long hours spent in the intimate discovery of shores and dunes.

But no matter how well-felt the observations and interpretations written here, I acknowledge the impossibility of representing the Holy Island of Lindisfarne to the full satisfaction of those whose home it is. My hope is that my friends there – and Robert Henderson in particular – will accept this book as a fair token in exchange for the gifts the island bestowed on me.

ONE

INSULA SACRA

The Heugh to Chare Ends

THE villagers of Holy Island have welcomed visitors in ever-increasing numbers throughout this century. Few escape the notice of Robin Henderson, Lindisfarne's oldest inhabitant and its 'unofficial' bird warden, who often stands on look-out where the road enters the village beyond the Chare Ends. His field glasses tucked navy-style under his arm, he notices the comings and goings of all and sundry. Who knows what flotsam and jetsam will come in with life's tide today?

In summer, when the sea's tide recedes, an endless stream of traffic off-loads holiday-makers, historians, ornithologists, pilgrims and returning islanders, each with a different reason for coming here. Among the folk who skirt the crowds round the ice-cream shops on Front Street or the Village Store in Market Place, Robin might spot one of his own relatives – his nephew, perhaps, or a distant cousin, or one of a number of friends who return frequently to the island. Many people

who visit Lindisfarne find themselves drawn
back, time after time, to wonder at the genius
of the place.

* * *

Their journeys begin with a sighting of the
island from afar. From the walled town of
Berwick, the Holy Island of Lindisfarne looks
like a full-rigged ship far out at sea. It takes
on the altered aspect of a forlorn, mystical,
castle-dominated place as the Edinburgh to
London train draws closer and drops out of
sight altogether at the level crossing behind
Beal Hill. When the route swerves towards
Bamburgh, the landscape appears flatter as it
blends with the open sandflats. A trick of light
might then transform the village of Holy
Island into a submarine's conning tower with
the Northumbrian coastline and the neigh-
bouring Farne islands under survey.

Tantalising glimpses from the train window
during journeys to and from Edinburgh was
all I knew of Lindisfarne until the day came
that I walked across the sands at low tide,
following the guide poles of the Pilgrims'
Way to the village. That journey was to be
the first of countless others, as, captivated, I
became a part-time island resident for several
years. Lindisfarne is laid down now in my
mind like the flight-path of a bird, and from
time to time a compulsion steals upon me to
return.

Approaching by road from the west a
breathtaking bird's-eye view reveals the island
as a rare jewel set in an opaline sea chased by

Northumberland's Kyloe Hills. From this height the traveller immediately appreciates the miracle of the island's survival within the vast expanse of the North Sea which rolls in on an endless front of foaming white breakers to surround it every twelve hours.

It is likely that both Aidan, arriving from the western island of Iona to found the seventh century monastery of Lindisfarne, and Cuthbert, travelling from Melrose to succeed him as Bishop of Lindisfarne, saw the island from the Kyloe Hills for the first time.

The naturalist Richard Perry's first glimpse of the island, too, was from this outermost edge of the Northumberland farmlands: a checkerboard of greens and gold petering out into sandflats as the road from the hills descends to the sea. The year was 1936 and, like me, the island was to hold him captive for several years during which he wrote *A Naturalist on Lindisfarne*:

> *The Holy Island of Lindisfarne! A chance port of call on the suggestion of a brother naturalist, a vaguely remembered name from a boy's history book .... To a naturalist it seemed a place of infinite possibilities ... but my appreciation was broken by my companion touching up his horse with a flick of the whip, and we clip-clopped down the long hill to a strip of salting and out over tide-wet mud to a line of poles, encrusted with barnacles up to the high-water mark.*

For centuries before the construction of the causeway road in 1966, several sets of direction poles guided travellers across the windswept sands. The only set left today was restored in 1989, complete with wooden refuge boxes: this is the ancient Pilgrims' Way which takes off at a tangent south of the bridge on the present-day causeway and follows the shortest route to the Chare Ends approach to the village. But the eroded relics of other direction poles can still be traced on Goswick Sand Rig, the likely safe-crossing point of fishermen taking the daily catch across to the Goswick Station and of early travellers bound for Berwick and the North by horse and cart or on horseback. Today's traffic is carried on a metalled causeway which was completed in two sections after rigorous tests proved the viability of a road which would be covered by the sea twice a day during high tides.

Richard Perry's dramatic crossing followed the line of the present-day causeway past the Snook and on to the village along the boomerang-curve of the dunes to the village:

> *The horse splashed deeper and deeper into a broad stream ebbing seawards, until at the halfway ford the water was swirling about its girth: for at high-water the sea, flooding in from north and south of the Island, met in this ford off the western arm covering the girdling sands and flats to a depth of seven feet.*

No islander would take a risk with the crossing, but visitors, ignorant of the force and speed which join the waters of the South Low and the Swinhoe Goat, sometimes do. And several cars are trapped by the tide on the bridge each year, their passengers forced to climb into the wooden refuge box. Here there is only one small comfort: a telephone through which to contact the police and Beal Garage and arrange for the salvage of the car (which in all probability is banging against the supporting poles of the refuge box with every gathering wave) when the tide recedes. On the highest tides, with nothing between the hapless incumbent and the eager sea but the swaying, storm-tossed mast of a refuge box, there would be every reason to send up a prayer to the maker.

Islanders have many tales to tell: of drownings and near-drownings, of abandoned cars and helicopter rescues, of people so enchanted by the aspect of the place from the A1 that they have turned off to explore it, unaware of the power of the tides and oblivious to the warning notice and tide-tables at the approach to the island.

Baffled by the extent of open sandflats and dunelands they have passed en route to the village, new arrivals can do no better than take their bearings from the grassy cliff called the Heugh. Literally 'the high place' of the island, this sixty-foot high wedge of dolerite rears up beyond Lindisfarne Priory with a view of the island's significant landmarks and landscapes and seascapes. Villagers climb up to take the air or walk the dog here. An old man might sit on the bench to smoke his pipe and marvel at the theatre of the sea below which, throughout a lifetime, has acted both as protector and destroyer of the place he calls home.

You can see almost everything from the Heugh. It is a wonderful spot for watching birds and, therefore, not so surprising that Robin Henderson and I should meet at the yirnin-whirls at exactly the same time on a late October morning. At either end of the tarmacadam path which cuts a diagonal over the field in front of the Priory (constructed in the 1950s for a visit of the Queen) are two old metal gates – yirnin-whirls – which squeak when turned by comers and goers, unless frequently oiled.

'Yirnin-whirls,' repeats Robin, relishing the sound. His Northumbrian voice sounds almost Scots as he says the words and we contemplate possible origins. The Scots 'girnin' or 'complaining' springs to mind. Complaining whirligigs. Yirnin-whirls. And I speculate about Robin's origins: Henderson, like a few other island names, could be Scots. Other island names trace far back beyond border wars and skirmishes.

Once there was a barometer at the yirnin-whirls near the Crown and Anchor pub. The fishermen, coming up from the harbour at night, struck a match on the gate-metal and held its light up to the barometer to catch the weather forecast. Robin looked after it for many years, but the last time it came down he decided it had been usurped by radio and television weather reports. It had had its day.

There is a curious expectant calm about this morning. Life itself seems suspended. Sunrise was a non-event, though it is brighter now as a grey cloud mass dispersing over Bamburgh allows a soft silver-gold fanlight to irradiate the sea below. As we climb the cliff the Northumbrian coastline and the mainland (which Holy Islanders call 'the Continent') unfolds its chequered beauty against the backdrop of the Cheviot which often hugs snow to itself from October to May.

Raised high on the Heugh the reward is an encircling view as fine as the eye could ever hope to see. This bird's-eye view sweeps over the poles marking the Pilgrims' Way to the village at low tide, snakes over shining sands past the Snook to the causeway and back over the ten hundred or so acres of dunelands and agricultural pastures which comprise most of the island. It alights on prominent features: the mysterious white pyramid at Emmanuel Head, Lindisfarne Castle, the harbour at the Ouse and the huddled village itself.

The island beyond the village is a fragile place where for centuries, season after season, part of the life cycle of thousands of birds has been enacted on shores and in dunes which host an astonishing variety of wild flowers. In today's nomenclature Lindisfarne is a National Nature Reserve; an SSSI (a site of special scientific interest); and a Ramsar site (a wet-land of international importance for wildfowl and wading birds).

Away to the south-east the Farne Islands are clearly visible. At night their Longstone Light sweeps the sea as if to answer a similar beam from St Abb's Head beyond the amber town lights of Berwick away to the north. St Cuthbert's Isle lies west of the Heugh, facing the Ross Beacons and the Old Ferry House at the end of the pale beige sweep of Ross Sands, with Bamburgh Castle rising in the distance from the sea, a mirror image of Lindisfarne Castle.

Robin asks if I have heard about the accident. No, I have just arrived. He measures his tone to tell me that the tragedy happened two days ago, at around nine thirty in the morning. For the first time in over twenty years a man was killed by gunshot meant for wildfowl out on the Slakes.

He describes how he was standing where we stand now, in the shelter of the ruined chapel on the Heugh, where the horizontal beam has fallen from a wooden cross. The rubble walls of the ruin make a good place to rest the field glasses on lengthy watches. The stones on the ground raise Robin high enough to see over and they have been polished smooth and shiny from decades of his standing there.

Robin Henderson, who has witnessed many accidents and deaths caused, one way or another, by the sea, and who has himself saved more than one life, heard the shot and knew at once that something dreadful was amiss. He points to a place over the sands to show me where, through his field glasses, he could see the gun-punt away out on the apricot-coloured Slakes, where the tide had left a few silver rivulets to mark its passing. Only one man was visible in the punt-gun, instead of two, and the wildfowlers' catch, a good one of widgeon and mallard, lay forlorn on the sands.

Within an hour the dead man and his traumatised friend had been brought ashore.

Robin's next words echo my thoughts. This terrible accident will bring the issues surrounding wildfowling to a head again:

'As you know, some are for it, some against. Those against will try to stop it now,' he said.

There are no wildfowlers or punt-gunners to be seen this morning out of respect, perhaps, for the man who has so lately lost his life. But there is a curious absence of birds too, apart from eiders on the Long Ridge and some swooping gulls. A bent figure harvests whelks from the rocks at Steel End. Four seals rest high-and-dry on the sandy Swad. Godwits feed gracefully along the tideline by St Cuthbert's island. A small group of shags mimics the sentinel stance of the Ross Beacons.

The pale-bellied Brent geese Robin hoped we might see are not there, although they have already arrived from Spitzbergen to overwinter in the area. These visitors from the Arctic tundra almost died out in the 1930s, partly because the tidal flat eel grass, *zostera,* which is their main winter food, was blighted by disease. But both geese and *zostera* have recovered and straggly low-flying formations of up-tailed Brents feeding at sea are common enough sights off the island now.

Nothing much stirs as we scan the seascape before us, until, suddenly, a dark cloud of bar-tailed godwits flits fast into view; it splits ranks, forming two clouds, each rapidly changing direction. His field-glasses sweeping the sky, Robin spots the spur to the action. A peregrine – *falco peregrinis* – scud missile of the skies. But, with more than a godwit on its mind, the falcon continues its fifty mile

an hour raid up the Slakes towards the causeway and the godwits head west.

Fishing boats, rounding Castle Point for
the harbour with the lobster catch, denote
the time of day. It is almost lunchtime. We
wander round the monuments of the Heugh
before returning to the village: the coastguard
station, flagstaff, cockpit, war memorial and
seventeenth century ruins known as Osborn's
Fort.

Recent archeological evidence suggests
the Heugh was once a thriving place: struck
flint, charcoal, sheep bones and what may be
a hearth are recorded below the ruined fort.
There are also the remains of a number of
small buildings which may date from Anglo-
Saxon times – geophysical survey techniques
indicate a buried wall, ditches and, east of the
coastguard station, a rectangular foundation.
The archeologists, who work on Holy Island
for several weeks every year, have speculated
that since this feature lies close to a doorway
in the outer court of the Priory, it may be the
ruins of the very watchtower, mentioned in
Anglo-Saxon sources, which received the
signal of Cuthbert's death from a beacon on
the Farnes.

Today's village is a neat, even a prim place,
honed down to essentials which facilitate lives
perpetually accompanied by sea winds. Even
on the balmiest summer day a breeze plays
on street corners and rustles the sycamores
in village gardens. Its summer gardens
burgeon with flowers and chances are that
Eddie Douglas, a near-contemporary of Robin
Henderson, will be hanging over his garden

gate near the post office, proud to relate the progress of his blooms, to chat about the weather and this and that.

Around two hundred people, including 'weekenders', live in the solidly built stone village houses. Tourism and fishing are the island's remaining industries, and it is greatly to the credit of Holy Islanders that, as the fishing has declined, they have directed the development of tourism, striving to strike the balance between income they need to survive here and the fragility of the island's ecology.

The sea, though, is the ultimate protector of its unlikely gift, ensuring that incomers arrive when the tide is low – but go away again, leaving the island at peace with itself.

* * *

Many visitors are surprised that there is not more to see of the island's Golden Age, that period of intense spiritual, evangelical and intellectual flowering when the fame of Lindisfarne's monastic community spread throughout the western world. Indeed, very little is known about the physical appearance of the monastery which developed between the seventh and ninth centuries.

However, the archeologists of the Lindisfarne Excavation Project, based at the University of Leicester, are making attempts to reconstruct that early community by exploring the features of today's village as well as through chance finds during recent excavation work and their knowledge of other early Christian monasteries in Britain and

Ireland. The Hiberno-Scottish foundation of Iona is particularly relevant, since its daughter house of Lindisfarne is likely to have been constructed on a similar model.

Iona, like other early Celtic monasteries, was enclosed by a prominent feature known as the *vallum monasterii*, a boundary bank which delineated the monastic territory from the rest of the world, both spiritually and physically. This sizable boundary area might have included gardens or home fields as well as the monastic buildings, and it is likely that the present village of Holy Island encompasses much of the site of the early monastery. Its street patterns, roads and features enclose an area comparable, although slightly smaller, to the boundary *vallum* on Iona where there is evidence that the enclosure is not all of one period.

And so the visitor to Sanctuary Close, or Priory Lane or St Cuthbert's Square, might feel a frisson of certainty that the feet of Aidan and Cuthbert once walked beneath his or her own, and might sense a link with the golden period when Holy Island was called *Lindisfaronaea*, its greatness spoken about throughout medieval Europe.

Its Celtic name was *Metcaud* or *Metgoit*. Its Norman name, *Insula Sacra*, the Holy Island, was used in official papers and manuscripts from the eleventh century. Celtic names, Latin names, names to conjure with. *Insula Sacra Lindisfarnensis*: the first part, 'Holy Island', is clear; where the name Lindisfarne derives from is not. *Lind-on*, though, is apparently Old English for water and *farona* for island.

There are other conjectures about the origins of the island's name which will doubtless occupy visitors for a long time to come, though the matter, like its weather, is hardly likely ever to be settled.

Village names, though, are another matter. The names of island families, which go back for centuries, are staunchly carved out for posterity on the headstones surrounding the Priory Church: Wilson, Allison, Selby, Lilburn. There was a time when a handful of surnames covered the island population, and nick names, acquired in early childhood, were kept for a lifetime to distinguish one family member from another. This tradition persists today when even incomers may be nick-named. The island's liberal councillor, who until recently also ran the post office with his wife, is known as Red Ian; Clinker, Wonker, Bones, Dancer, Crow and Poppy are traditional nick names, some of which attach to today's islanders. Robin Henderson's nick name is Cock Robin. Other names stand as memorials for islanders long gone: Jenny Bell's Well, Jock Mathison's Bank, Lilburn's Cottage, Julie's Burn.

I take my leave of Cock Robin near his pigeon loft off St Cuthbert's Square. Then I walk past the post office, Fiddler's Green and the Priory Church to the path which skirts Mustard Close and Easter Field to the limestone shore beside the former Lifeboat Station overlooking St Cuthbert's Isle. A seven-part dolerite dyke underlies Holy Island and runs almost due west through Kyloe to Cornhill. The most westerly part of the island dyke is under St Cuthbert's Isle, at Hob's Thrush. The next section is the Heugh; another emerges low, east of the harbour, only to reach its greatest height of a hundred feet at Beblowe Crag and peter out at Scar Jockey on the foreshore, with Plough Rock and the Goldstone out to sea, both hazardous spots for mariners.

The rocky shore which runs below the Heugh to the Chare Ends holds evidence of earlier domestic life in multi-coloured china fragments of Victorian design. There are bits and pieces of rusty ironmongery from old beds, utensils, tools and lamps. For the cliff here was the traditional town dump, the convenient repository of the old tossed-out in favour of the new from medieval times to the present: Jenny Bell's Well midden. One dark winter afternoon recently, the island's electricity supply was cut off. In order to carry on its business the post office borrowed an oil-lamp from a weekender who was also asked about its operation: 'You see, we've forgotten how to work them. We all threw the oil lamps over the cliff in 1957 to celebrate electricity coming at last.'

The archeologists found that much more ancient rubbish had been thrown over an underlying older cliff, in-filling a natural fissure of the rock to give the present cliff its surprising height. They recorded bronze age pottery similar to shards discovered in other parts of north-east England, as well as a bronze, socketed, side-looped spearhead from the middle bronze age. Here, too, are several medieval dumps packed with wild bird bones, cattle horns, fishbones and shells from mussels, winkles, limpets and whelks. Also unearthed was a surprising range of pottery fragments: imported wares from Germany, the Low Countries and France, leading the excavators to the conclusion that, despite being off the beaten track, Lindisfarne was once part of the vast trading network of the North Sea.

Did Cuthbert drop off his rubbish here, en route to his little offshore sanctuary? St Cuthbert's isle has a number of interesting ruins above the high-water mark which were first investigated in the nineteenth century. It is easy to walk to the island in the steps of Cuthbert at low tide. The small chapel, now marked with a cross, has an attached western chamber which dates from the late middle ages. The mound nearby is probably an early Christian cell.

Beyond Jenny Bell's Well, the causeway road comes into view at the Chare Ends where it enters the village. In summer the full tide can be smooth and warm and deep enough to swim in: Lindisfarne's 'lido', where deck-chairs and picnics unfold on lazy summer afternoons.

The naturalist Richard Perry, harking back to the 1930s, described a pre-war island community of some 250 men, women and children living in 83 houses, four inns and the Castle:

> *Since the late 'twenties the catering trade has benefited enormously from the introduction of motor transport to all sections of Britain's population, and by the Islanders' own initiative*

*in running a fleet of high-chassied Ford-cars
between tides for hire, supplementing and
replacing the picturesque, but slow-moving,
horse-brakes and traps in which visitors formerly
had to cross the sands.*

*By the late 'thirties the boom in bed and
breakfast had affected the well-being of almost
every family on the Island, even the fisherfolk:
'for their daughters and those sons not in the
boats could find employment directly or indirectly
in this trade ... somewhere in the middle
'twenties the islanders' general standard of
living began to rise and has continued to rise
ever since, stimulated latterly by the numerous
material benefits that the war has brought to
the lower-incomed workers'.*

It was not always so. Although the book
on Lindisfarne was firmly closed after the
monastic community departed across the
sands, leaving a few, perhaps, to eke out a
living alone, it was opened again in the
sixteenth century with *Reports to the Crown*
following the 1537 Dissolution of the
Monasteries:

*The island hath in it a little borowgh towne,
all sett with fishers very poore, and is a market
towne on ye Satterday, howbeit it is little used
... the more parte of the towne is now decayed
in howses, and yit the tofts and crofts where the
howses did stand remayne.*

By the mid-seventeenth century the entire
island was estimated to be worth just over
one half as much as the rabbit warren at the

Snook. The cottages would be primitive with walls of thick mud and plaster, roofed and floored with sods of earth with small windows to keep out the elements and a large hearth to huddle at for warmth.

But a degree of prosperity did reach Lindisfarne in the eighteenth century. W. Hutchinson's *History and Antiquities of Durham* (1794) recorded that 'the village consists of a few irregular houses; two or more of which are inns. [It] has been improved of late years by the building of several new tenements ... [and] become a place of great resort'.

Fifty years later, despite a reported lack of cleanliness (from gentrified perspectives), Lindisfarne was a thriving Victorian resort, documented by Walter White in his book *Northumberland and the Borders* (1859) and in a *Natural History of Eastern Borders* by Dr George Johnston who stayed on the island for a fortnight in 1854.

Extracts from their accounts betray not a little condescension towards lives less luxurious than their own, but are fascinating nevertheless:

> *Whitewashed cottages, some of them retaining the primitive thatch, constitute the bulk of the dwellings, while among those of better style appear nine inns or public-houses ....*

> * * *

> *In the village, or the 'town' as the natives proudly call it, there is a square bestrewn with unsavoury rubbish and the condition of the*

*streets accords herewith, implying that public
cleanliness has not yet grown to a habit.*

* * *

*A stroll through the village disclosed very
sensibly the nature of the principal occupation
of the natives. In every street heaps of the shells
of the mussel and limpet are collected before the
doors, and mixed with the refuse of the fishing
lines, and with the household ashes, etc. They
do send forth a most foul and fishy smell,
evidently agreeable to the senses of the house-
holders.*

* * *

*Around almost every door lies a heap of floats,
and lines, and queer-looking oilskin garments,
and ample sou'westers hang on the walls. And
at times a few men, wearing thick sea-going
jackets, and boots up to their hips, take their
way down to the beach.*

* * *

*Here and there you may see a potato-plot, and
a garden with a few flowers and vegetables, and
in sheltered corners an elder-tree in blossom;
but of other trees there is a general lack; and
judging from appearances most of the population
are of* [the] *opinion that all the land is good
for is to grow vegetables in.*

Walking towards the village up the Chare
End Road past Lindisfarne's 'suburbia' –

detached and curious houses with names like 'The Bungalow' and 'The Chalet' entirely made of wood – and the red-brick Lindisfarne Hotel whose tea-time garden fills with summer visitors, the island's Edwardian period plays on the imagination.

Early in the century, when the train stopped at Beal, entire families would disembark to be picked up by horse traps and transported across the sands to stay for up to a month at the Lindisfarne Hotel, the Manor House or one of a number of inns and bed and breakfast establishments which are still in business today. Then, cream linen suits or navy-blue and white clothing were worn (often in striped combination) with sun-stopping panama hats. Croquet was played on the lawn, while teas with cucumber and crab sandwiches were served before a spot of fishing or, perhaps, a gentle round of golf on the nine-hole course (now extinct) which was opened in 1907.

That period began a hey-day for the island when, in 1901, Edward Hudson (founder of *Country Life,* the magazine which opened the doors of private houses to curious readers for the first time) stopped over on a motoring tour and decided to convert Lindisfarne Fort on Beblowe Crag. The castle is near the top of the island visitor stakes attracting 50,000 visitors a year, close-second to the Priory which claims around 100,000.

My walk to the Heugh with Robin, followed by a scramble along the rocky shore, has been contained by the falling and rising of a tide. Apart from some island children playing on their bikes in Front Street, and the odd villager hastening to get something last-minute before the store closes, the village is empty; cars, buses and vans have departed in a well-timed evacuation across the causeway. Once again, the sea recreates Lindisfarne as an island.

TWO

BETWEEN THE TIDES

The Straight and the Crooked Lonnins

ITS tides define it. The island survives in the grip of the sea. Twice every 24 hours the sea throws a glimmering girdle round its sandy perimeter. It takes five hours to complete the cycle of rising and falling tides which steal in from the far North Shore through the Swinhoe Goat and between the Harbour and Ross Beacons and south through the North Goat and the South Low. In all but neep tides, which leave Goswick Sand Rig, Beal Sands and the Slakes uncovered, Lindisfarne is cut off from the mainland for two hours before high tide and three hours after it.

In summer there is nearly always a cluster of folk at the approach to the causeway or near the bridge, watching, waiting, wondering at the meeting of the waters which take Lindisfarne hostage only to release it again and again. Man is both fascinated and uneasy when his assumed power over nature is threatened. In the matter of the rising and falling of the tides which surround the island twice a day, man has no influence. They rise and fall

and he must wait and watch with the sobering realisation that he is but a grain of sand after all.

This is the tranquil time when the island returns to itself – a traffic-free zone of tangible peace broken only by the sounds of a village going about its pedestrian business and the birdsong in its lanes and gardens. The tranquil time, when the tide rises to sever the island from the mainland, is when you will find Holy Islanders exchanging news and gossip at street corners, in the market square, from the open doors of their houses and in shops devoid of tourists.

When the tide is in, there is time to notice a house at the top of the village with curtains the colour of the yellow wallflower springing, scented, from the crevices of its garden wall. It has a built-in wooden side porch, flush with the stone façade, painted the same green as the wallflower leaves. Its architecture is redolent of another era. This timeless tide encircled era belongs to no specific century or decade, but is unique to the Holy Island of Lindisfarne cut off by the tide.

The house belongs to the Royal National Lifeboat Institution, whose presence on the island is kept alive only in the memories of those who participated in its operation and in a litany of the names of its lifeboats on a plaque outside the Priory Museum: *Grace Darling, Bombay, Bedford, Edward and Eliza, Lizzie Porter, Milburn* and *Gertrude*. When the lifeboat services were withdrawn in 1968, islanders were left with a deep sense of loss consoled only by the knowledge that theirs had been one of the first lifeboat stations in Britain and one with an almost incredible record: since 1865, 205 launches were made from Holy Island and 336 lives were saved.

Robin Henderson spent forty years with the RNLI as the only full-time crew member of the Holy Island lifeboat and still wears its enamelled badge dead-centre on his seafaring cap. In reality he acted as wireless operator, mechanic and crew member all rolled into one and was invited to stay on in the house after the lifeboat went out for the last time.

There are not many these days who can claim his pedigree: Holy Islander born and bred. He wears the snug-fitting navy-blue cap, a fisherman's gansy and, depending on the weather, a navy-blue raincoat. His gear conveys the same sea-related sense as the clothes worn by sea-faring islanders at the turn of the century who stare out at you from sepia photographs in the bar of the Crown and Anchor. They stand there, lined up beside the lifeboat, pulling up the fishing boats or marvelling at some huge creature lately landed from the deeps.

Cock Robin notices the fall of a sparrow, the arrival of the first fulmar back to the Coves, the vicious swooping of black-back gulls after young eider on the Slakes, an area under his particular guardianship. He carries a wealth of island lore and stories within, mostly unrecorded. His weather-beaten face dances as he tells them. Tales of the sea, of wrecked cargo boats, lifeboat rescues, narrow escapes. Tales of birds, of merlin and plover, of shelduck nests at the Snook. Tales of war-

time and peacetime on the island. The advent
of invention and the newfangled, of electricity
and the causeway. Tall tales and small talk.
The stuff of island life.

Today's wildlife rekkie takes us out of the
village down the Straight Lonnin, an earthen
lane which leads to Nessend above Coves
Haven: to that high point where the island's
history began in a scatter of shaped flint and
stone left behind by mesolithic, neolithic and
bronze-age man. We pass the steading of the
near-derelict St Coombs Farm, where a gaggle
of geese, with assorted duck, cocks and hens,
preen, strut and cackle. Sometimes the motley
fowl-mob takes a wander up the Straight
Lonnin, the geese guarding the way against
intruders with an impressive rush of spreading
wing.

The Straight Lonnin skirts fields of grazing
sheep edged with a bent and wind-twisted
avenue of scrubby hawthorn, alive with
carmine-tipped male linnets and spice-hued
greenfinches. A rough road this, which peters
out after serving its purpose about three-
quarters of a mile from the farm, it leaves
pedestrians to find and keep to a track over
open dunes to the sea.

The Lonnin's purpose seems to have been
to service the area of agricultural and industrial
land beyond the village. To the left is the area
called Lower Kennedy, now deserted of human
habitation, the undisputed territory of several
pairs of breeding lapwings. From the twelfth
to the nineteenth century here was a centre of
thriving industry whose constructions are
only visible now as tantalising hummocks.

Crumbling limekilns on the dunes ahead stand as memorials to the industry that endured for five centuries at various points on the island. They burned seaweed for fertilisation in pits at Lower Kennedy, too, as early as the thirteenth century. In 1845 when workmen were constructing a tramway to the limekilns at Lower Kennedy, they exposed the foundations of two buildings which may have been the dwellings and storehouses of kelp burners and found two coins from the mid-ninth century.

The second half of the nineteenth century was the island's industrial hey-day, the sounds of its manufactories ringing out all along the tramway embankments which encircled the quarries at the Coves, the kilns at the Castle and here, at Lower Kennedy. There were five cottages for 'foreign' workmen just north of the dunes here and two more behind Sandham Bay.

Richard Perry, almost certainly party to oral history, writes:

> *The works joiner and the blacksmith lived in these two* [cottages], *the latter being remembered more especially because his wife wore a single garment of sacking .... There were ten or eleven inns to cope with the demand for liquor, and if this be thought a tall story I can name nine of them – the Ship Inn, the Brittania, the Fisherman's Arms, the Selby Arms, the Plough Inn, the Iron Rails, the Northumberland Arms, the Castle Hotel and the Crown and Anchor – and can verify the site of a tenth, the Cambridge House.*

Street and inn brawls were common then.
And although some of these inns survive
alongside newcomers, to this day no policeman
has been able to live on Holy Island. The story
is still told of the policeman called Constable
Joe Smoke who imprisoned the drunken
ancestor of a present-day islander and was so
harried by the villagers that he took refuge on
the roof of the jail. Twenty mounted police
came riding across the sands from Berwick
the next day to quell the disturbance.

* * *

We might prefer to take another route out of
the village during the spring and autumn
migration. It is then that 'twitchers' abound
up and down the Straight Lonnin, their gear
hauled about them like antennae: elongated
telescopes and a great variety of binoculars.
Robin steals me a sideways glance, as if I did
not know. 'Twitchers is birdwatchers. They
wait at the end of a phone for news of sightings and rush here, there and everywhere, to
Holy Island from every corner of the land.'

But the spring migration is over and it is
to the eider nurseries that we are going on
this glorious late-June day. The air is heady
with the scent of purple clover once grown
with silverweed near the Links, abundantly,
as crops. Crossing the Links where the 1907
golf course was situated, we enter the dunelands called the Quixes. Feeling large and
conspicuous as we move through its soft,
untrammelled space, I do my best to observe
and to emulate Robin's measured, stealthy

gait. It is not unusual to spot a fox here. In the warm air of the close stacked dunes their odour lingers. Their droppings are everywhere. Several pairs breed at the Snook, but they sometimes take a jaunt up here, in search of tastier morsels than the staple, rabbit.

Robin confides that he knew the naturalist Richard Perry who picked up a lot about the island's birdlife, out and about, like this. 'I taught him some things in the beginning,' he remarks modestly. Perry spent time on the island, a good deal of it on wartime lookout duty between 1936 and 1945, and married an island girl. It was during spells of coast-guard duty near the fulmar cliffs above the Coves that he developed a special interest in the bird's flight pattern.

According to Richard Perry, the first fulmar was noted on Lindisfarne in 1879 and a year later the first British colony outside St Kilda was established on Foula. Fulmars were observed only four more times on the island before the end of the century, after which the east cost of Scotland was rapidly colonised, and by 1928 this fulmar cliff at the Coves was firmly established.

Standing above the Nessend cliffs, as we do today, Richard Perry observed the birds on many visits and recorded evocatively:

> *With the last hull in the convoy gone down behind the Farnes and my watch-mate on the Castle battlements holding his peace at the other end of the 'phone, I had the leisure to reflect.*

Could it be, he wondered, that by returning

to a cliff on which it had bred in previous years, the pale fulmar was responding to a 'memory'?

> *But had I not erred in regarding the Fulmar as a Sea-bird that came to land only to breed? Was it not, rather, a Land-bird that went out to sea after the breeding season? .... I began to see how it might be possible to bridge that void between breeding-cliff and wintering ocean-periphery. There were not two Fulmars: the Fulmar of the cliff and the Fulmar of the ocean; but only the cliff-Fulmar going out to sea in August to complete its moult and recuperate from the long months devoted to its main purpose in life, the reproduction of its kind. And no matter how far, or for how long, the Fulmar planed over the sea, it carried with it the memory of the Island cliff and also of its fly-line: a memory that would bring it back home the way that it went out. There was no void, no periphery: only a continuous flight from and to the breeding-cliff.*

The tide is fully in. It is a perfect summer day, warm and sunny, fanned by a gentle breeze. Nothing stirs but the fulmars which gently whoosh past in patrol of the clifftop ledges where parent birds attend their young. Soon the clifftop will become a flying school for the chicks which bravely fall into air-pockets for the first time, to learn the characteristic sustained fast glide of their kind. And in the bay below, the silky-coned heads of numerous grey seals rise almost impercep-tibly from the water to peer at our passing.

Curious markers in the topsoil above Nessend Quarry alert us to the recent presence of the archeologists whose island-finds have revealed new sites from all ages: the first monastic settlement, a prehistoric scatter here and an outstanding medieval farmstead at Green Sheil.

Lindisfarne was once a low hill in a vast mainland plain. In the days of the earliest hunter-gatherers the coastline was two or three miles out beyond the North Sea which races for the shore like Elgarian 'brave white horses' gathering speed as the tide reaches its height. Standing here on a carpet of sea-thrift it takes a dramatic leap of the imagination to reclaim that landscape from the sea, to envisage the great sweep of this ocean as a vast coastal plain peopled with encampments of hunters and to realise that this high cliff was once their hill fortress, affording a good view of their territory, many miles in circumference.

Yet they were here. Their legacy is hundreds of pieces of humanly struck flint, chert, quartz and chalcedony, some in arrowhead form, found by the archeologists.

Walking towards Sandham Bay, the sea all around us, I am struck again by the miracle of the island's survival. Hundreds of square miles of the coastline which once surrounded it disappeared forever into the jaws of the sea, leaving only this wind-battered tract of coarse-grassed dunes, rocky outcrops and mudflats. This tidal island we call the Holy Island of Lindisfarne: a sanctuary for wildlife, the focus of all kinds of pilgrimages down the centuries; the exquisite gift of a rapacious sea.

Ahead of me, Robin brings my musing to an end with a gesture of flapping hands. It is time to conceal ourselves. He drops full-length onto his stomach, one hand protecting his binoculars, the other pulling his wiry body stealthily forward to a position between clumps of marram grass at the edge of the bluff.

Silent and hidden, we observe the secret world of the eider nurseries on the great sea-slab pavements below. The birds have come here from their breeding grounds at the Farne Islands and Ross Sands. The females are so colour-coded with the rock as to be at first invisible. The colony is spread in groups, females with chicks: small darker-coloured fluff-balls. Some adult birds sit, some sleep, their heads twisted round to beak-nestle in the back-feathers. There are at least fifty birds here.

It is some time before an adult female stirs and waddles up to sip and preen at a rock pool, followed closely by her gaggle of six chicks. She leads them to the water's edge where the receding tide produces gentle ripples. Other females do the same and soon the sea is a swimming pool for young eiders and the air is filled with their gentle 'coo-roo-ing'. Here they learn the joys and dangers of the medium which they must master to survive.

At this stage, the eider drakes are nowhere to be seen. The early training of the chicks is left to the mothers who form creches and co-operate with the others in their demanding task. Later, the fathers will come to sit and swim near the colony. It will be three years or so before the juvenile males have put on the distinctive black-and-white plumage which makes them almost unrecognisable from their seniors.

It is impossible not to think of Cuthbert in connection with the island's Eider population. While other monks sold the eggs and stuffed their pillows with eiderdown, Cuthbert, according to accounts of his life, fed them with pulses from his own mouth and from his barley crop. He encouraged the ducks to nest around his oratory hermitage on the Farne Islands which can be clearly seen from the spot where we lie hidden now. Cuthbert was, Richard Perry observed:

> ... a metaphysical naturalist ... moved by the same spirit that twelve hundred years later made William Darling, keeper of the Longstone, strew sand upon the naked reef at the base of the Lighthouse, that the Terns might alight and sun themselves around him, to the delight of his gentle daughter Grace.

Perry continued:

> To his contemporaries and successors Cuthbert's command over the Eiders seemed miraculous. It is only in the present century that the patronymic of St Cuthbert's Duck and its abbreviated form of Culvert Duck have begun to fall in disuse among north-east coast fishermen.

But most Holy Islanders today will tell you that eiders are Cuddy's Ducks; the link between bird and saint endures.

It might seem strange then that, by and

large, the monks of Lindisfarne displayed no
interest in recording the wildlife around them;
that they were not naturalists in that sense.
In vain did Richard Perry search monastic
statements of accounts to be rewarded by
nothing more interesting than entries like:
'Twelve Maulerds hanging in the larder.'

The interlaced bird illustrations of the
Lindisfarne Gospels have excited much
scientific discussion. Since Holy Island is so
rich in wildlife, surely the monks had specific
local birds in mind? Alas, ornithologists have
discounted the possibility that the decorative
illuminated birds are either the cormorants
or shags which they most resemble and which
love to stand, spreading their wings to dry on
the rocks at Coves Haven. 'Nevertheless,'
persists Janet Backhouse in her book, *The
Lindisfarne Gospels*, 'it is hard not to see in
them some reflection of the Cormorant family,
seated in characteristic attitude on the rocks
with necks and beaks proudly extended and
with the sun striking the gleaming iridescence
of their feathers.'

Surprisingly enough, scant references
speak of Holy Island's flora and fauna until the
late eighteenth century when Thomas Bewick,
the great craftsman and illustrator, modelled
exquisite woodcuts of eider and pochard duck
for his *History of British Birds* (1805) on island
specimens. 'A countryman by birth, a man of
ripe wisdom, and a true naturalist,' says Perry;
'Bewick was the first, after Turner, of that
distinguished line of Northumbrian naturalists whose achievements no other county in
Britain can rival.'

There is every reason to be grateful to Richard Perry for the dedicated hours he spent combing books and records to document Lindisfarne's important naturalists in his wonderful book *A Naturalist on Lindisfarne* which remains the ornithological 'bible' about the island's wildlife.

For Perry the 'modern era of Ornithology' arrived with the publication of Prideaux Selby's *Illustrations of British Ornithology* and his *Catalogue of Birds hitherto met with in Northumberland and Durham* in 1831, with William Hewitson who published his *British Oology* at this time, and with two brothers – John and Albany Hancock. Hewitson and the Hancock brothers made frequent visits to the Farne Islands where William and Grace Darling collected bird's eggs, flowers, shells and geological specimens for their private collections which formed the basis of Newcastle's Hancock Collection.

True, the first ever British Field Club, the Berwickshire Naturalists' Club, held a meeting on the island in 1833. But Lindisfarne continued to be curiously ignored in the records of outstanding birdmen until C M Adamson changed all that with his four *Books of Scraps*, crudely illustrated with pen-and-ink drawings of waders and wildfowl. But a later contemporary of Adamson's outshone them all. 'Abel Chapman,' trumpets Perry, 'strides like a colossus over the Northumbrian scene':

> *Between them, Adamson and Chapman shot, collected, and observed on the Island and its surrounding slakes and seas, from swad-box,*

gun-punt, and fishing-coble, for close on a
century, presenting us, in unbroken continuity,
with a unique record of the Island's Wildfowl,
Waders, and Seafowl, from the dawn of modern
ornithology to the present era.

[Chapman was] well-known to the fishermen and wildfowlers of the Slakes and Fenham
Flats as to the shepherds and keepers on the
wild fells and mosses of Cheviot and all the
vast wilderness of the Border. Patriot Artist,
Writer, Naturalist, Wildfowler and Punt-
gunner, Angler, Big Game Hunter and Preserver,
Explorer in a score of lands for Newfoundland,
Spitzbergen, and Scandinavia, through Jutland
and the Iberian Peninsula, to all four quarters
of Africa, this extraordinary man, with his
almost superhuman powers of physical endurance,
had few superiors .... The range of his knowledge [included] almost every kind of European
and African game, big and small, from
elephant to salmon, and several hundred species
of the birds of two continents. No wonder that
his hardly credible knowledge occasionally led
him into small errors of identification or habit.

George Bolam, though not of Chapman's
stature, was meticulously accurate:

He was the last of the great all-round naturalists bred by the Berwickshire Naturalists'
Club and sired by Drs Johnston and James
Hardy, whose literary industry and encyclo-
paedic knowledge of all branches of natural
history make one's brain reel whenever one has
cause to turn over the pages of the club's
Transactions.

Chapman and Bolam both knew the island's first resident naturalist, George Watson, whose scientific records, compiled between 1920 and 1924, enabled Richard Perry to produce a *Systematic List of the Birds of Holy Island* to 1945. The list includes 256 species plus 35 'probables, possibles [and] doubtful sub-species' and birds spotted within a ten-mile radius of Holy Island.

Approaching the Lough, which has all the grace of a landscape watercoloured by a Japanese master, Robin agrees that Richard Perry would have appreciated the bottle-green painted hide erected here recently to the memory of another birdman by his friends and family with the support of the then Nature Conservancy Council, recently re-named English Nature.

> *A pleasant spot, the Lough – that six-acre sheet of fresh-water, now stained pink with bog-bean and amphibious polygonum – at which to sit awhile and watch the young Shoveler Duck, hardly bigger than Teal, spinning around suspiciously when hawking Swallows skim past their heads, and the homely Moorhen – homely only in the sense of their common distribution over the British Isles, for their inscrutable ways have inspired the most profound philosophical study of animal mentality.*

Perry's detailed observations of birdlife remain unsurpassed and still strikingly accurate, particularly with reference to wild-fowl and waders. Here and there, though, the reader notes that times have changed. The sycamores are no longer by the Lough side, the rooks less prolific:

> *From now until the nesting season* [Rooks] *visit the Island daily. In the evening they gather on the brine-corroded sycamores of their ancestral rookery at the Lough, but towards the darkening they depart and, flying south, pass low over the Heugh with soft caws and queer crooning and sotto voce grating, beating out over the Slakes to their roosting woods on the mainland.*

In his turn, Perry noted changes since even earlier authors recorded their observations:

> *The elms, like the alders, birches, black poplars, and rowans noted by Johnston, perished in the dessicating gales a generation and more ago, but the grove of sycamores, which must have been planted not many years before Johnston's visit, still stand fast and put forth their pestilence-stricken leaves each spring – tho no Blackbird whistles merrily now the onstead has fallen into ruins.*

We have crossed that open coastal strip between Emanuel Head and the entrance to the Crooked Lonnin which is so dominated by the Castle's northern aspect. On such a day there is something truly munificent about the air which marries the fragrances of dune and pasture lands with those of coast and sea. This sensuous air on the edge of the island carries a message to the wanderer about his humble origins and extraordinary evolution from minuscule sea creature to hunter-gatherer and beyond. For all that, Lindisfarne reminds you, again and again, that you are but a grain of sand.

Robin holds open the gate at the Crooked Lonnin for me to pass through: 'He married a local girl you know.'

Who? Richard Perry. Ah, yes.

As we wander up the lane I remind Robin of Perry's conclusion to his chapter about Holy Island naturalists in which he mentions two young fishermen, James Lilburn and Robin Henderson, whose interest in birds, and fauna and flora in general, went 'further than the mere shooting and collecting for the pot or for purposes of identification'. 'Up till now,' he wrote, 'neither has kept written records, but, on their return from overseas service, we may look forward to his history of the Island's ornithology being kept up to date for many years to come.'

The Crooked Lonnin brings us back to St Coomb's farm, past the only two houses outside the village apart from the Snook. I wonder if, when Robin goes, we will ever know his like again. Perry mused thus about Selby Allison, a great local whose memory has become almost a legend with Holy Islanders. He was Abel Chapman's favourite puntsman and during the war he was still spry enough to spy, through his telescope over his garden wall, the Brent Geese on the Swad. Robin often does just that, keeping tradition alive.

'The younger fishermen and puntsmen are hardly to be distinguished from their fellow Islanders,' lamented Perry. But he failed to have sufficient faith in the devotion of Robin who has kept records for half a century. And, who knows, though I have heard older islanders lamenting the unruliness of today's young and their lack of interest in tradition, there may be one or two among them who will pick up the songlines Robin must one day leave behind him.

THREE

SPLENDOUR OF JEWELS AND GOLD

The Pilgrims' Way

O N a particular day in spring the weather will be perfect. The shining tidal pools of the Slakes, which bear the Pilgrims' Way, will mirror blue skies and scudding clouds. But even if the day should chance to be grey and wet, soaking the hundreds of folk descending the hill from Beal towards the Pilgrims' Way, in spirit they will remain undaunted. For they are pilgrims and the day is Good Friday. They walk barefoot, some share the burden of huge wooden crosses on their shoulders. They sing that their faith will remain constant 'come wind, come weather'.

They congregate from all over England and from Scotland. They represent several denominations and have come to Lindisfarne, one of the holiest places in Britain, to recommit their faith in this spectacular annual act of worship. They are joined by a few others, of no particular persuasion, but who sense, perhaps, that something missing from their lives might be retrieved, like a jewel in the sand, by walking the Pilgrims' Way to the village of Holy Island at Easter.

They honour a tradition of pilgrimages to Lindisfarne which began in earnest after Cuthbert's death, as, in his lifetime, the saint predicted they would. These were pilgrimages made by believers intent on seeing for themselves the places where prayer had been answered. But, long before Cuthbert, the early Celtic Christians made 'white pilgrimages' to sacred places like Lindisfarne. These were heroic journeys, like the one Cuthbert himself undertook after he received the vision of Aidan's death when he was a shepherd on the Leader Hills near Melrose.

At the Chare Ends the pilgrims are welcomed by leaders of their various denominations. Some will spend the weekend at the Marygate and Cambridge House; others in overflowing hotels and guest houses. In the evening the ancient Priory Church of St Mary becomes the focus of an ecumenical service of readings, music and song. A pageant follows as the congregation bears lighted candles down to the beach opposite St Cuthbert's Isle where, dressed in white hooded robes, the servitors of St Mary's light a symbolic bonfire.

On such a night, and in such circumstances, it is not difficult to conjure up the spirits of Lindisfarne's two great religious heroes, Aidan and Cuthbert. It was Aidan who founded the monastery at Lindisfarne around AD 635, close to the stronghold of his patron King Oswald at Bamburgh. Aidan came from Iona in response to a request by

Oswald (who had been baptised into the Christian faith at Iona) for missionaries to convert his heathen Northumbrian subjects. As historian Arthur Bryant describes, they were a lawless mob:

> *They loved fighting, their poetry, chanted in the mead halls of their chieftains as they sat feasting at long tables, is full of the clash of the 'hammered blades', 'the serried bucklers', 'the shields of linden wood', of 'arrows sleeting like hail'. They loved the symbols of death and carnage; the raven who followed the host, his beak dripping with blood, the hungry hawks hovering over the battlefield, the funeral pyre hung with shields and helmets round which the companions of the fallen sang the joys of war and the warrior virtues.*

The first deputation of Ionian monks to Lindisfarne failed. The monks returned to Iona perturbed, saying that the Gospel would not be heard by the crude and cruel Northumbrians. Language, too, was a barrier; but on the second mission led by Aidan, King Oswald was on hand to translate Aidan's Gaelic, and slowly the Lindisfarne monks became fluent in the dialect of Northumbria. Lindisfarne must have reminded the monks of Iona where, similarly, the sea acted as a visible barrier between the monastic community and the outside world, as well as providing a partial defence against invaders.

Cuthbert's birth coincided with the arrival of the Ionian missionaries to Lindisfarne. When he himself came to the island after

Aidan's death in AD 651, the community was well-established.

Two detailed accounts of Cuthbert's life were written within a few years of his death in 671. The first, written around 700 by an unnamed Lindisfarne monk and known as the *Anonymous Life of St Cuthbert,* was expanded some five years later in a metric version by the Venerable Bede and again around 720 as the *Life of St Cuthbert.* A very young Bede is said to have met Cuthbert towards the end of his life. Certainly, there were people living in Northumberland at that time who had known the saint well and whose evidence was included in both books.

The finer details of Cuthbert's life recorded in these accounts contributed to the hero status he was accorded down the centuries. Within their pages we have evidence that he took all the steps necessary to make him a legend even in his own lifetime. As a shepherd on the hills near Melrose 'he had seen angels ascending and descending, and in their hands was borne to heaven a holy soul, as if in a globe of fire'. The holy soul was Aidan, who on the night of Cuthbert's vision – 31 August 651 – died in a humble shelter at Bamburgh.

The teenage shepherd responded to the vision by entering the monastery at Melrose which Aidan had established as a satellite of Lindisfarne; and, some 13 years later, Cuthbert was appointed Abbot of Lindisfarne itself. His outward challenge was to implement Roman ritual there, according to the decisions of the Synod of Whitby. He acquired a reputation for piety and the possession of miraculous powers. His personal quest, though, was for at-one-ness with God. He was, says Bede, 'aflame with heavenly yearnings'. He craved solitude as a means of coming closer to God and retreated, first, to the tiny hermitage of Hob's Thrush, now called St Cuthbert's Isle, which is cut off from Lindisfarne at high tide. Later he constructed a hermitage on Inner Farne where he could see nothing but the sky, 'thus restraining both the lust of his eyes and of the thoughts, and lifting the whole bent of his mind to higher things', according to Bede.

Cuthbert's subsequent return to Lindisfarne strengthened the monastic institution and brought life and vitality to the community. He performed miracles and, by both the anonymous account and Bede's account of his life, was a warm-hearted yet practical man who had an Assisi-like way with animals. It was in Cuthbert's honour, sometime in the 690s, that the magnificently illustrated Lindisfarne Gospels were created.

* * *

To the pastel-coloured dune world of Lindisfarne the monks brought vivid colour: primary blue, yellow and red pigment from plants and minerals, held ready within opaline cusps of purple-blue mussel shells, to be mixed for the decoration of the Lindisfarne Gospels. To the short-day darkness of the winter island at the edge of civilisation, the monks introduced one of the world's greatest masterpieces of manuscript painting, a vivacious affirmation of life, bound in jewels and gold.

Eadfrith, Bishop of the Lindisfarne Church, originally wrote this book for God and for Saint Cuthbert and – jointly – for all the saints whose relics are in the Island. And Ethelwald, Bishop of the Lindisfarne islanders, impressed it on the outside and covered it – as he well knew how to do. And Billfrith, the anchorite, forged the ornaments which are on it on the outside and adorned it with gold and with gems and also with gilded-over silver – pure metal. And Aldred, unworthy and most miserable priest, glossed it in English between the lines with the help of God and Saint Cuthbert.

The words are Aldred's, the 'unworthy and most miserable priest', who added an Anglo-Saxon translation to the original Latin text around the middle of the tenth century, as well as to the end-page quoted above which names the four men who made the Lindisfarne Gospels.

The script which Eadfrith chose for the main text of his Gospels – *insular majuscule* – was developed in Ireland and passed into Northumbria through Iona and the Irish missionaries. It was written with broad nibs cut from reeds or quills, both easily obtainable near the island.

The pages are of folded sheets of *vellum*, probably costly calfskin, carefully prepared to form a good writing surface and near-white in colour.

The writing area was pricked out with a stylus or sharp knife, leaving round and wedge-shaped marks. The text area was also marked out before the writing began in darkest brown ink with added carbon from soot or lamps.

The large and subtle range of colours used in the decoration of the gospels derives from recognised sources, which Janet Backhouse lists in her own book, *The Lindisfarne Gospels*: red and white lead, verdigris, yellow ochre, yellow arsenic sulphur, kermes (from Mediterranean insects), gall, indigo, woad and other plants, a fine range of pinks and purples from the fruits and flowers of the turnsole plant, and exotic blue *lapis lazuli* from Badakstan in the foothills of the Himalayas which 'must have passed through many hands before reaching the monastery in Northumbria', and small amounts of gold paint.

The richly decorated Lindisfarne Gospels were intended for ceremonial use, a visual symbol of the Word of God which the missionaries had carried to their converts. Its creators were not isolated geniuses, though. As Janet Backhouse points out:

> ... the seventh and eighth centuries were among the most artistically productive in the whole of English history, especially in Northumbria, where the two or three decades on either side of the year 700 were truly a golden age. From this period we still have many surviving examples of book painting, jewelry, metalwork, sculpture and building in stone. There is also a literature, both in Latin and in Anglo-Saxon, and ample evidence of outstanding scholarship, especially in the works of the Venerable Bede.

Colour and irradiation are eagerly sought by

the winter visitor to the island. Most of them hope that the advent sun will shine through the live-long shortest days of the year as a sort of visual mantra of hope for the year to come.

On one visit, as darkness drew in, the weather forecast coming in on the car radio made me shudder for fishermen at sea. 'Gale warnings … Thames, Tyne, Rockall … north west six to gale nine; Fortes, Cromarty, Forth, Tyne, Dogger Bite … gale nine decreasing five later.' The car made it through the last waters of the falling tide, over the causeway, through piles of soft seaweed and juddered to a halt in the village square.

A famous crossing, albeit a fantasy one, appears in the first minutes of Roman Polanski's black comedy film set on the island: 'Cul-de-Sac'. The old jalopy in which the two hapless heroes are happily driving along the causeway suddenly judders to a halt. One of them leaves to get help at the castle; the other falls asleep in the car and wakens to the shock of the incoming tidal waters lapping round its doors.

That reminds me of my first New Year on Holy Island when the winds had been high for days, distorting tides that were already full. We just made it to the village, fording the waters at the Chare Ends soon after midnight on Hogmanay. The car juddered to a halt 'Cul-de-Sac' fashion on the road leading to the the castle and all its electrics cut off. We overheard some islanders passing in the darkness remark (not surprisingly): 'Aye, there's some that doon't know what they're doin'. Had a few many a doon't doot.'

Two hours later we had been welcomed at several houses, the car had dried out and we drove away heady with the experience of Lindisfarne first-footing where habits are similar to those in Scotland: there is the first-footing, the lump of coal and the cake or shortbread; but not the giving of a coin. There is something, though, which I have never heard of happening elsewhere. After the men return home in a more or less sorry state a day or so after the New Year bells, on the second day of the year it is the women who go on a good-humoured galavant from house to house, decorating themselves with baubles and tinsel from Christmas trees, as if in some primitive ritual. They proceed to the Lindisfarne Hotel for supper and thence to the pubs where the men might, or might not, come to winkle them out.

Once the women went to the house of a 'weekender' who was upstairs in bed, recovering from Hogmanay excesses. Alarmed by what sounded like a rabble approaching, he hid in the bedroom cupboard. But the women were upstairs like a flash and they carried him out into the village square dressed only in his underpants, teasing him mercilessly. He has not returned to the island for New Year since.

The Crown & Anchor, where my bed was booked for the night, was closed. I tugged the door handle and rang the silent bell to no avail, tying my tartan scarf more firmly against the taunting wind, stamping my feet against the cold. Then I remembered that under no circumstance would any inn open until seven o'clock. The deserted village seemed to ignore my plight. Enveloped in darkness, I felt utterly alone. But it would be better to walk than stand and freeze. Here and there, diffuse light seeped through curtains, indicating life within. I imagined people singing along with 'Songs of Praise' or, more likely, watching a television game show on 'the other side'.

Curlews cried over the darkness beyond Fiddler's Green. On the edge of the village I was relieved to see light in the darkness: stained glass windows illuminated from the lights within the Priory Church. The church looked inviting, the coloured windows glowed like motifs in an advent calendar. Partly out of curiosity, partly out of a distinct need for warmth and comfort, I found myself opening the great wooden door, tiptoeing across the sanctified ground and slipping into a back pew with four or five elderly women whose habit of coming here throughout a lifetime would be broken only by death.

Here was time to absorb the beauty of the place: roseate renaissance arches, the soaring architraves, the rich needlework of the kneeling cushions, the ordered wooden pews. The vicar was addressing his advent theme of hope, light in the darkness, as symbolised by the birth of the Christ child.

Near the entrance to the church, pamphlets are for sale which detail the lives of many saints associated with Lindisfarne, finely distilled by hagiographers: Aidan, Columba, Cuthbert, Finan, Colman, Hilda, Wilfred, Eadfrith and all the others.

The rational facts of the history of the

British Church which these pocket-size references contain are fascinating. But something much more exciting is scarcely hinted at within their pages. Lindisfarne played a leading role in deeper and more mysterious truths which trace far back beyond Christianity to the so-called Dark Ages. In this almost forgotten Celtic twilight, the island was a powerful node on the spiritual network of the early monks, or Druids. These people were unselfconscious ecologists whose lives expressed a combination of attraction to and awe of the natural world, an attitude of humility which modern man is at last beginning to recognise as vital to the planet's survival. The Celtic monks set up monastic schools in Ireland and the Western Islands of Scotland to celebrate the potency of the divine presence in nature through music, poetry, art and science.

It is doubtful if anyone in the village took much note of a lone pilgrim who arrived by car in 1968. He was not sure why he turned off the A1 and headed for Holy Island, just making the crossing before the tide came in. He meditated in the chapel and later came to the realisation, as others have done, that it was here, at Lindisfarne, that Christianity took the wrong turning, after the clash between Celtic and Roman Christianity at the Synod of Whitby in the seventh century. The lone pilgrim was the American philosopher William Irwin Thompson, who in his impassioned spiritual travel book, *Passages About Earth*, quotes Professor Needleman's account of the circumstances surrounding the clash:

The clash had been developing during the episcopate of Finan, who succeeded Aidan at Lindisfarne; and it became unavoidable when Oswy in 655 slew Penda of Mercia, the last defender of heathenism, who had stood between the stream of Christianity coming down from Iona and the stream pressing northwards from Canterbury. Colman, the third bishop [of Lindisfarne] *inherited the dispute when Finan died in 661. King Oswy's sympathies were with the Celtic Church in which he had been brought up at Iona, but his queen and her chaplain followed the usages they had been familiar with in Kent. The confusion in the royal household was such that Easter was kept twice .... Aware that the Easter divergence in 665 would be even greater than usual, Oswy summoned the Synod of Whitby in 663 or 664 at the monastery ruled by Hilda, pleading that all who served the one God should agree to observe one rule of life. Colman claimed that the Celtic traditions went back to St John; but Wilfred, a former disciple of Aidan, who had visited Rome and adopted Roman usages, laid emphasis on the folly of resisting the unique authority of St Peter: 'The only people who are stupid enough to disagree with the whole world are these Scots and their adherents the Picts and the Britons, who inhabit only a portion of these two islands in the remote ocean.'*

The king had evidently already made up his mind, with a view to unity and peace in his own house, and with a smile he announced his decision in these words: 'If Peter is the guardian of the gates of heaven, I shall not contradict him. I shall obey his commands in everything to the best of my ability: otherwise, when I come to the gates of heaven, he who holds the key may not be willing to open them.'

The Synod of Whitby was ostensibly to do with the date of Easter and other disputes such as differing styles of liturgy and monks' tonsures; but, as Irwin Thompson eloquently outlines, its root causes lay in the far deeper split between European and Celtic consciousness:

> *Two roads crossed at Lindisfarne; one went to Rome through Wilfrid, the other went to Iona through Colman. Aidan had come to Lindisfarne from Iona, and it was at Iona that Aidan's teacher, St Columba, had created a centre of esoteric Christianity. It is small wonder that after the failures of the Synod of Whitby Colman and his monks left Lindisfarne and went back to remote Iona. It would be nice if we, too, could go back to Iona to find some old document like the Book of Kells that would give us instruction in Christian forms of meditation, but the inner* [esoteric] *techniques are rarely committed to writing. They pass from realized man to realized man, and if we are to rediscover them in the present, it is not to some exercise in archeology that we must commit ourselves but to those living places where the culture of man is not cutting violently against the grain of the universe.*
>
> *We have been so turned around by our society that we no longer feel the stars turn. We have become so used to feeling religious only when we are uncomfortable and full of pride for having*

bothered to go to church at all that we no longer remember that religion was once a force that created civilisation out of barbarism and inspired almost all the great works of art in history. The power of cosmic myth is still with us, but it is not to be found in churches or elegant drawing rooms where clerics and academics sip sherry and discuss a fine point in the latest fashions of theology. When the unconscious and the conscious come together in a culture, the energies are not polite, civilized, or comfortable.

Patently, man urgently needs to access these energies once more. The hope that he may one day succeed is held out here in Lindisfarne, is inherent in its air and atmosphere, in the beauty of its fragile landscape, its flora and fauna. Here one may feel the stars turn. Hope is the island's gift to a wayward world.

A long time ago, two roads crossed at Lindisfarne. It is possible to trace back to find the other road at the fork. That other road is ecological, esoteric and universal. As a tribute to the insights the island inspired, Irwin Thompson founded the Lindisfarne Association whose New York headquarters provide a node on a vibrant network of biologists, economists, musicians, artists, poets and philosophers whose touchstone is the truth expressed in Bamford and Marsh's book *Celtic Christianity*: that if the Celtic Church had survived, the fissure between Christianity and nature which has widened down the centuries might not have cracked the unity of western man's attitude to the universe.

* * *

The island councillor, Ian Macgregor, leaves his pew to take up the collection in an exquisitely embroidered velvet bag as the organist plays 'Nun Danket'.

'It's good to see you,' he whispers. 'In the right pew, too.'

As he moves away towards the altar for the blessing of the collection, the penny drops. I was with the Scots in the back pews, wearing my tartan scarf! As in many border churches, the congregation here is divided: Presbyterians in the back and Episcopalians in the front pews. The organist brings the evening ritual to a close with a spirited rendition of 'Sleepers Awake' and the congregation trickles out, each with a greeting from the vicar, and disappearing through the lych gate into the darkness.

* * *

Awaking in the dawn hush next morning, I realise that the gale has blown over. The yirnin-whirls under the bedroom window squeak and clink as the first of the fishermen starts the day. I watch him cross Sanctuary Close towards the harbour, a colourful figure in the dawn light: grey-knit cap pulled over red curls, bright blue overalls, soft green jerkin, yellow waders folded down with large cuffs below the knee. Soon the advent sun steals over the horizon to light the world.

The pub had gone like a fair the night before, with islanders and a few visitors attracted to its fire-lit bonhomie. One or two fishermen were there, now brimming over with rascally charm, now lapsing into reminiscence tinged with regret.

'Things are not the same any more. Not like they were. When I was young we always looked up to the older men and in them days they would have chased anyone that misbehaved straight off the island.'

Incomers are still occasionally chased off the island for transgressing a few remaining unwritten rules, mainly to do with young island women and the fishing. Once the powers-that-be tried to install a policeman in their midst and the tale of his unceremonious dispatch is told with relish. True, there is little wise counsel for the young now, but that applies to communities everywhere in the western world. Perhaps though, the falling away of tradition is more keenly felt within insular communities. Holy Island evinces 'social problems' in all its age-groups, like everywhere else. The other side of the secure familiarity which the island holds out to those who call it home is an almost tangible frustration to do with a real, or imagined, sense that the world turns without it.

The fisherman drains another pint, lights a cigarette and gazes into the fire to develop his next theme. 'Even the fishing's gone off. Must be pollution. Something like that. Or the ozone layer. There's none of that seaweed you used to pull up with the fish. *Lam ... laminaria.* Something like that it was called. It was a' stringy, like bootlaces, and its root was attached to a rock. You hardly see it now though.'

By and large the island community feels itself removed from the small Christian community whose profile, these days, is low and concerned more to offer hospitality and retreat to appreciative visitors, at Marygate House and Durham House, than to be much involved in island life. Such schism might well trace back to the first monastic community which subjugated island inhabitants to its service, and, in all probability, though there is no certain proof, abandoned them to eke a living without support after the monks fled the island.

Several accounts emphasise the lawless side of island life in the eighteenth and nineteenth centuries. A particularly disturbing version of schism was made by a young Methodist, William Ferguson, in 1782. At the age of twelve he moved with his parents from Eye-mouth to Holy Island:

> *The people of this place were mostly smugglers, and the children remarkedly wicked! Of these I soon learnt to curse and swear, and to glory in my shame. I learned to tell lies for sport, to play at cards, to dance, to work the greatest part of the Sabbath Day: and to make a mock at all religious people, saying they were all hypocrites. And in this deplorable condition I remained, till I was near 20 years old.*
>
> *So I continued fast asleep in the Devil's arms, till one day as I was working in the shop with my father, my mind ran upon a match of drinking and dancing in which I was engaged to join in the evening. Suddenly I heard a voice from heaven saying, 'What if thou shouldest*

drop down dead in the midst of the dance!
Wouldest thou go to heaven?'

I said: 'No. I am not fit for heaven.'

I immediately felt I had passed sentence
upon myself; and that if I went not to heaven
hell was my portion; light broke in: I was filled
with horror: I saw myself hanging over the
mouth of hell, by the little thread of life.

In the evening my company came in, to
carry me to the dancing. To their great surprise
they found me reading the Bible.

They asked my father and mother, 'Are you
not willing he should go with us?'

They said, 'Yes; but we think he is not
well.' They said, 'Come, we shall soon cure him.'

'Do,' says another, 'and I will carry his
fiddle.'

I looked at them and said very mildly, 'If
you do carry me, I shall be of no use to you. For
a dance I will not dance this night: and a tune
I will not play.'

They stared and left me.

As soon as the inhabitants of the Island
found that I would not drink, swear, or work
on the Lord's Day, they were violently angry, so
that I could hardly walk the street, for a mob
setting upon me. And my father and mother
insisted on my working at my business on the
Lord's Day. But I told them, 'No: never more;
I will sooner have the flesh torn off my bones'.

Poor William Ferguson. He would be
welcomed on the island today, and no one
would bat an eyelid about whether he worked
on Sunday or not, though he would have to
translate his skills as a watchmaker into

something more relevant to his survival.

As I retrace the Pilgrims' Way towards the Causeway, concepts like Good and Evil, Heaven and Hell, the Devil and God, seem totally disconnected from a brilliant world of sun suspended over the shining pools of the Slakes where ecstatic shorebirds dance out the shortest day. But my lengthening shadow, darkly cast on the pale sands, reminds me that it was precisely the contrast of dark against light in the deserts of the Middle East which induced early philosophers to speculate about the presence of both dark and light within the soul of man.

I retrace the steps of the monks who, a hundred years after Cuthbert's death, fled in the wake of a Viking raid, taking the saint's relics and the Lindisfarne Gospels which honoured him. The four volumes 'in all their splendour of jewels and gold' were later swept into the sea during a storm. Miraculously, they were recovered unharmed on the sands at low tide.

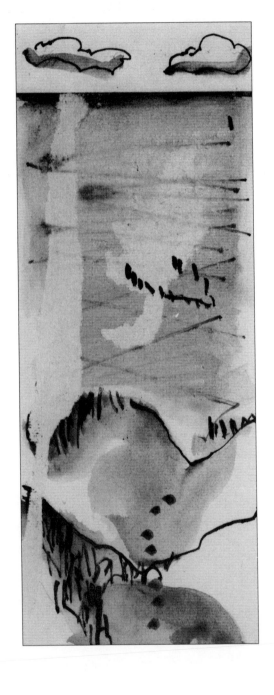

FOUR

TERRIBLE PORTENTS AND FIERY DRAGONS

Emmanuel Head to Green Sheil Bank

AT seven-forty precisely, a refulgent, blood-orange sun steals over the horizon between Lindisfarne and Bamburgh. Its first glowing shaft smites bedroom walls up and down the Northumbrian coast, much as solstice suns impact on ancient Celtic stone chambers. This experience, repeated again and again, is one of the rewards offered to folk who endure the darkness of the long winter months ahead – Holy Island's 'morning glory'.

The sun soon reaches its zenith, irradiating the island and the surrounding sea. The sky is a cerulean blue ceiling above scudding pink-tinged clouds, the waters of the Slakes and the Swad liquid silver, the sugary-sand apricot-pink. An unusually abundant crop of samphire at the Snook Wideopens has turned carmine in its dying: fine fare for barnacle and greylag geese in the weeks to come.

Recently arrived redshanks dart and twist over the causeway, their elation unaffected by the occasional passing car on its way to the village. I, too, feel intense, almost ecstatic, anticipation at being on the island again in October. October is one of the most exciting months of all, when migratory birds stop over and the first geese, ducks and swans, arrive to overwinter.

For the past three days gale force winds have pounded the Northumbrian coast, scattering birds like leaves and leaves like birds, tearing off roof slates, tossing down trees and branches, soughing through the Kyloe woods and descending with gathering ferocity to the sandflats. Half-way to the village a mini-*hamsin* has blown huge piles of sand off the Slakes to pile up on the causeway, forcing cars to move cautiously until a JCB comes from the mainland to clear it off later in the day.

There is a lull in the weather this morning, but it will not last. On the other side of the island the sea is still whipped into a fury of curling, foaming waves, over ten feet high at the bar. As I leave the post office with the milk and papers, I see Robin's spry figure beating a track towards his house. When I catch up he fixes me with a considered gaze: 'You should have been here last week.'

I know. The migrants must have had a field day, resting and feeding undisturbed under the thick band of fog which had drawn a veil over the island for most of last week.

'The twitchers was a' here: a sparrowhawk lifted out a yellow-browed warbler. A lot of folk saw it. It was in the papers, you know.'

Yes, I should have been here, but I have at least memories of other Octobers, more balmy and less foggy than this, when the island was alive with the sight and sound of passerines; when birdwatchers appeared in posses surrounding the wall of the garden at Snook House, binoculars trained on the sycamore trees, hopeful of a sighting of rarities like the red-breasted flycatcher or pine grosbeak.

'I'm walking out to Sandham,' I say, hoping that Robin will want to go too. He is wearing the same familiar hat, with its RNLI badge pinned on dead-centre, but different gear today: a short green waxcloth coat, a bright blue polo-necked sweater:

'Waders,' he suggests.

Yes, I want to see the wader birds. But Robin has been at his pigeon loft most of the morning. It's getting on for dinner time and he's tired of the wind. Instead, we go into his house and he stirs up the fire. Invited to inspect the capacious larder, I congratulate him on sufficient overwinter supplies of tins and dried goods to feed an Arctic explorer. Then he pulls up a chair for me, closer to the fire. Sandham Bay must wait. Robin has tales to tell.

'I took a peregrine last week.'

'You what?'

I watch incredulously as he re-enacts the event. His hands move like an Indian dancer's as he indicates that he wants me to imagine the bird at the other side of the room; then his wiry body steals towards it like a cat, and he pounces, enfolding the imaginary bird in his arms.

'It's great claws went for my chest but I managed to hold it off and got it to the house.

It was sitting on the bluff: eyes yellow, talons yellow, beak marked with yellow, a female with these cheek moustaches. Its breast feathers was a' scrawny, its rib cage was skinny. It was worn out, ill or old. I don't know what. But a marvellous bird.'

He measured it up on the table here in the room, he told me. It had a wingspan over 16 inches. It died before he could send it off for scientific examination. I told him about the dead sparrowhawk I had found on the causeway after the winds, bleeding badly from the beak. I wondered how it had died.

'All things must come to an end. Even the strongest birds of the air must die,' was all he said.

It is early afternoon when I emerge and set off towards Emmanuel Head, the navigational beacon which takes on an almost mystical aura in certain weathers. It was erected in 1828 by Trinity House to take its place with other markers on the Plough Rock, the Heugh, in the fairways and on the mainland south of the island, to offer ships safe access to and passage round Lindisfarne.

The hide at the Lough provides welcome respite from the quickening wind which brings down immature gulls and mallard ducks to play on its riffled water. The waters of the lochan have receded to a pond, more or less in the middle of its space, revealing rushes and autumn-brown grasses. A few moorhen, a lone coot, pochard and a little grebe. Before long a human autumn visitor and his dog arrive at the hide. The man has been watching birds all week and reports the first arrival of sanderling at Sandham Bay.

In exchange I offer news of a flock of barnacle geese, strikingly black and white against the gold-stubble field north of the castle, and go off bent into the wind, uncomfortably aware of its cold fingers fumbling for any entry through my layers of clothing. Sometimes Holy Island's winds are so prolonged and incessant that you long for silence and stillness, for calm and balm before winter sets in.

From the bluff at the Emmanuel Head end of Sandham Bay, all is movement on a grand scale. High tide waves plunge headlong and furious towards the shore and reach their turning point almost at the base of the dunes below me. A fleeting glance reveals a mass of waders: oystercatchers, ringed plover, turnstone, dunlin … and, yes, sanderling. But the sand-laden winds whip and sting my face, eyes and hands, and force me back to an entirely different world behind the bents: almost calm, almost balmy.

Movement and rhythm are ever-changing. In the ten minutes it takes to reach the other end of the bay, the sun has broken through, the wind has calmed a little on the receding tide. It is possible to sit in a sheltered spot not far from feeding waders, darting back and forth with the tide, through silvered rivulets seeping out of seaweed shoals thrown up by the tide. Redshank rise and twirl in windpockets. A dark-brown chorus of meadow larks accentuates the gleaming world of the bay, waiting for the seaweed to dry out to produce the insects they relish. The feeding waders are too busy for more than the occasional brilliant, piping song.

Passing high above the stone-paved eider nurseries, against the wind, I think of Robin and summer days, and that he was wise not to come today, though he is with me in spirit. Perhaps Robin was thinking that he is well past his three score years and ten when he remarked: 'I don't know that I'll ever get to know you like I did Richard Perry.' Ah, well.

Back in force again, the gale makes it impossible to get anywhere near Nessend where the island began, at least in man's knowledge of its history. It forces me back, sideways now, threatens to blow me off my feet. The sky has become dark and menacing and it begins to rain. This rough day suggests a Viking landing. I can almost visualise the Longboats emerging over the horizon to be borne like dragons to the shore. Words from the *Anglo-Saxon Chronicle* seem to sound in the wind:

> *793. In this year terrible portents appeared over Northumbria, which sorely affrighted the inhabitants: there were exceptional flashes of lightning, and fiery dragons were seen flying through the air. A great famine followed hard upon these signs; and a little later in the same year, on the 8th of June, the harrying of the heathen miserably destroyed God's church on Lindisfarne by rapine and slaughter.*

True, there is no lightning today. If the *Chronicle*, put together a hundred years or so after the event, is to be taken literally, the first significant Viking landing on British shores happened at a different time of year. No matter. A feeling of portent and turmoil is present today in the relentlessly crashing breakers against the stones and boulders of Coves Haven.

Our ancestors had much more fertile, poetic and ecological imaginations than we, though, and I prefer to believe that the language the chroniclers used to describe this monstrous violation of one of Britain's most treasured spiritual heartlands was largely symbolic. The attack, fraught with such surprise, shock and terror, had impact akin to lightning strikes and fiery dragons flying through the air. The longships, of course, had prows carved and gilded to resemble dragons, their teeth bared in snarling menace. They were designed to terrify, as these lines from *King Harald's Saga* reveal:

Men will quake with terror
Ere the seventy sea-oars
Gain their well-earned respite
From the labours of the ocean.
Norwegian arms are driving
This iron-studded dragon
Down the storm-tossed river,
Like an eagle with wings beating.

They would come on the tide, trapping the largely monastic population: simple, defenceless, trusting people in the main, for three or four hours. There would be nowhere to hide and no possibility of leaving the island. Anyone reading accounts of the event, and who has experienced the isolation of Lindisfarne on a rough and cold, wet, windy day, might imagine the terrifying experience of being trapped by the unknown.

Here was easy prey for the Vikings: a calculated strike on a totally undefended church and monastery, which would be known to contain wealth in the form of coins and treasures, as well as humans to sell or ransom and livestock to live off.

No one knows for certain where they landed. But, hugging close to the shelter of the landside dunes, as the North Shore offers glimpses of itself bearing a ferocious, foaming sea, galloping unhindered over the miles between here and Goswick, I put my money on Green Sheil: the bay at Green Sheil, where the rocky paves of the Great Whin Sill peter out. Here is a natural haven where muscle-bound men might countdown the oars till, at last, their monstrous warships touch *terra firma*.

The word 'Viking' came into English usage only in the nineteenth century and tends to be associated with northern Scandinavian peoples, literally 'sea-inlet dwellers'. The upstarts who swooped down on Lindisfarne and other parts of Britain at the time were mostly Danes. They followed the flight paths of migrant birds. They arrived exhausted and wind battered, but their impact was enormous. It marked the beginning of the end of the island's monastic community.

Nothing like these Viking longboats had ever been seen before and they came with the speed of lightning. Their arrival sent shockwaves throughout Europe. Alcuin, the distinguished Northumbrian scholar and, later, abbot of Tours, was at the court of the Emperor Charlemagne when news of the raid of Lindisfarne reached him:

Lo, it is nearly 350 years that we and our fathers have inhabited this most lovely land, and never before has such a terror appeared in Britain as we have now suffered from a pagan race, nor was it thought possible that such an inroad from the sea could be made.

This invasion must have seemed as improbable as a moon-landing to Britons who knew nothing of a technology which could produce graceful craft of curved oak planks with astonishing shallowness of draft: less than one metre across, even when fully laden with men and goods and gear. This stream-lined new technology allowed the Vikings to sail up rivers and into bays which would ground more conventional warships. They could even be pulled by the crew overland and through hilly passes with the aid of wooden rollers under the hull.

There is nothing much underfoot as I follow the shelter of the bents to Green Sheil. The grass sward or turf has been ravaged by rabbits right down to the sand. Their profuse droppings form a rough covering mingled with dried stocks of dumpy sea-centaury and the tall stems of ragwort stripped by tiger moth caterpillars. Because the water table is near the surface in these 'lows', plants like creeping willow, bog-pimpernel, grass of parnassus and carpets of marsh-orchids grow here profusely in season.

There is no evidence that the village remained inhabited after the departure of the monks. But a century after the Vikings landed, the remote and secluded area called Green Sheil was. There is an early medieval settlement here buried deep in a dune-circled sward: several buildings, linked by enclosing walls and yards.

The site might never have been re-discovered but for the industry of workmen constructing a waggonway from the lime-kilns to the North Shore in the middle of the nineteenth century. The large stones they found here were just what they needed, so they quarried them and used them for tracks. Despite the fact that they found two Saxon coins, the importance of the site was not recognised until 1980, and since 1983 an extensive programme of archeological field-work and excavation has been carried out every year by the University of Leicester's department of archeology and St David's University College, Lampeter.

Green Sheil, say the archeologists, is one of the best rural settlements of the period in the British isles. It is a secret, dune-protected place, very near the sea and the marine resources of the foreshore, but also near the estuary on the narrow waist which links the Snook lands to the rest of the island.

It was occupied during one of the least-known periods of Northumbrian history, between the troubled ninth century and the construction of the priory in the late eleventh century. The excavation and analysis of the site is ongoing, the results to date are important and complex. What can be discerned of the spreads of walls and the large loose stones suggests the remains of a number of buildings. The archeologists expect that only one or two will turn out to be actual dwelling houses and that the site will be identified as a large farmstead rather than a hamlet or a village.

Every year, in late summer, a group of dedicated diggers makes its own encampment here, meticulously dry-sieving deposits with the tools of their profession, some of which are sent for further laboratory analysis to remove small seeds and bones. Finds already made include the complete skeletons of a cow and a calf, deer antlers, the remains of seal, whale and wild birds including the extinct great auk. In addition to the coins unearthed by the waggonway builders, a penny from the era of Aethelred of Wessex and two ninth century Northumbrian coins, known as *stycas*, and an Anglo-Saxon spearhead, have been discovered.

Beyond this mysterious ancient place, which in summer is carpeted with orchids and pearl-white grass of parnassus, a path leads through the dunes to the Sheil, a single habitation of a more recent era. Who knows now what its function was: a *sheil*, literally a shelter for a shepherd grazing a few animals? Or a fishermen's bothy? Whatever it was, its existence recedes from year to year as the remaining gable wall threatens to be buried under the sand forever. Or, perhaps not forever.

Over the last few years the high tides and strong sea winds have ravaged the dunescape here, bringing them down, flattening them so that flotsam and jetsam of all kinds – wood, plastic, glass, wire and tin – gather with piles of seaweed, nearer and nearer to the Sheil. Perhaps this process will continue to erode the sandbanks, displaying the building again in its ruined glory as a structure to be listed by the planning authority.

Behind the Sheil a path traces over to the causeway road. The wind has almost played itself out. The tide has receded far enough to allow me to walk briskly back to the village across the sands. I pick up a dead dunlin on the road, its purest-white breast plumage down-soft and almost black underneath with winter plumage, its legs astonishingly fragile and elegant. It still feels warm though it is quite dead: one of many thousands of birds brought down exhausted along these shores by the autumn gales.

I shape a litany in my mind for all those I have seen over the years – for guillemot and gannet, for redwing and redshank, for cuckoo and kestrel, eider and shelduck. Sometimes they have been struck down, not by the elements, but by a fox which has eaten out the soft fleshy parts and left the plumaged skeleton.

* * *

Between September and mid-February wild-fowling takes place on Fenham Flats, strictly controlled by permit issued by English

Nature wardens. The pursuit of punt-gunning was introduced on the Slakes by a Norfolk gunner in 1829. Local fowlers mastered the technique sufficiently well to obtain a score or more of Brents at one shot with the big gun two years later, Richard Perry records, adding: 'Now and again a bare record of some Duck or Goose obtained suggests what marvellous notes a naturalist in a punt might have recorded for a grateful posterity one hundred years later.'

Today's sad reality is that the old standards of sportsmanship, which took pride in skilled and carefully conducted sport, have become tarnished, with more uninitiated people clamouring to wildfowl. In 1961 the Wildfowl Conservation Committee of the then Nature Conservancy Council defined an area to be available for controlled wildfowling, a course which led to the establishment of Lindisfarne as a National Nature Reserve in 1964.

Although controversial, wildfowling is a traditional and legal pursuit, and English Nature takes the view that, carefully controlled, the sport is a useful management tool in which some 2500 birds, a tiny proportion of the total wildfowl population, mainly widgeon and mallard, are taken. All non-quarry species are totally protected and the shooting zone is flanked by sanctuary areas to which the birds can move to feed and roost undisturbed.

Eight gun punts are in operation: the four local outfits are launched from below the Heugh and those of visitors from the causeway near the Refuge Box. The punt itself is propelled towards the quarry by paddle or punt pole, and when it has been manoeuvred to within seventy yards or so of a group of birds, one of the two men in the punt bangs on its sides with his knuckles. Up goes the petrified flock, straight into a burst of shot some twelve feet in diameter, some to fall dead or wounded back onto the flats. An old twelve-bore shotgun, ironically called a 'cripple stopper', is on hand to put injured birds out of their misery.

Then the 'bag' is collected by the men, wearing wooden pattens or mud-shoes to stop them from sinking into the ooze. It is a point of honour that all shot birds are recovered.

There are signs that the islanders themselves have become less interested in wildfowling, and punt-gunning in particular – an attitude which the latest tragic accident is bound to reinforce. Shoulder gunning, certainly, seems more acceptable nowadays, less indiscriminate, fairer. The islanders have permanent fixed shooting-butts dug into the sea-bed out on the Swad: half-barrels, wooden boxes and even an old cast-iron bath in which to settle down on straw to wait for the widgeon to come in. This method of wildfowling has a certain morbid mystique about it, heightened, for me, by the sight of the shadowy figures of oil-skinned men emerging from their cars in the darkness at the Snook road end to dis-appear into camouflaged punt guns on the Slakes. Sometime later the put-put of the guns will be clearly audible. In a season the local bag may be about fifty birds, sufficient for the households and for the traditional island Duck Dinner held every season at the Lindisfarne Hotel.

The village ahead, perched high above the sands, reminds me of a submarine's conning tower. Behind me, in gathering darkness at the Snook road end, I can just pick out the lone figure of the nature reserve warden parking his tractor beside the caravan from which around six hundred wildfowling permits are issued each year, with leaflets where necessary on sportsmanlike etiquette and standards expected of wildfowlers.

The main English Nature Reserve office is at Beal Halt. The whole reserve covers 3500 hectares of dunes, saltmarshes and mudflats, some of the finest in Britain, from Goswick Sands in the north to Budle Bay in the south, with a stretch of foreshore at Cheswick Black Rocks.

In summer the warden and his assistant patrol the shores, laying down stones for nesting terns, reporting dead seals, erecting fences to halt dune erosion, spraying the mudflats to maintain a balance between the vital *zostera* and the menacing *spartina* grass. In winter he supervises the wildfowling, catches up on vast amounts of paperwork, reports and recommendations.

But winter is not far off now. Snow-bearing winds sometimes hamper the progress of the sea as it approaches the causeway. Then a congregation of bewildered oystercatchers might watch low-tide water turn to ice on the road before flying off in search of more predictable feeding grounds. Some years large deposits of snow have filled the approach road to Beal, cutting off Holy Island from the rest of the world for days at a time. More often, though, the salt-laden air melts ice and snow before it takes hold, a circumstance which encourages the winter arrival of thousands of birds from the Arctic tundra.

Walking to the village, I imagine how the island might look from the eye of a passing bird, owl or merlin perhaps. Some hawk-eyed observer or other might pick out pin-pricks of light from village streets, skeins of smoke here and there from its chimneys, an inordinate expanse of sand and mud flats, and the lights of Berwick, an amber necklace, ten miles north.

There are lights in the darkness all around me now, clusters of light and single lights reflected in an oily-dark sea. It is as if part of the milky way had fallen to earth. Beyond this darkness and these lights the North Sea continues to roll in a gathering frenzy whose only control is the insistence of the tides.

FIVE

CASTLE-SWIRLED CRAG

Castle Point to the Harbour

WHAT is left is what we see: this wind-battered tract of coarse-grassed dunes, rocky outcrops and mudflats. A sanctuary for wildlife, the focus of all kinds of pilgrimages down the centuries. The exquisite gift of the rapacious sea-place where man has left significant memorials to time's passing.

For such a small place, Lindisfarne's themes are on a grand scale: the early Christian roots which sanctify the island as one of the holiest sites in Britain; its legendary saints, notably Cuthbert, a hero of mythic proportions; its place in history as the site of the first significant Viking landing on the British Isles; its more recent history – Border wars and skirmishes, the brief flare of nineteenth century industry, the romantic Edwardian castle.

These threads and monuments of the island's history lure 500,000 visitors every year, but the restricted visiting hours imposed by rising and falling tides leave little time to

explore the rest of the island. Fortunately. For beyond the village lies a fragile place where, season after season, part of the life cycle of thousands of birds is enacted on shores and dunes which host an astonishing variety of wild flowers.

From the stone-scattered sward of Castle Point the eye sweeps over the island's significant backdrops: the limekilns, the Castle, the Harbour, the Priory, the Heugh. The solidly impressive limekilns, memorials now to an indigenous industry which, for a few decades during the nineteenth century, connected the island in trade and commerce with places as far away as Dundee. 'Foreigners' came from the mainland to swell the size of the village. The lime industry awakened the island to the industrial age and the bustle of the new in a flurry of expansion: the excavation of quarries, the building of waggonways to transport the lime, and a jetty at Chare Ends to dispatch it.

Lording-it behind the limekilns, Lindisfarne Castle rises on its basalt-plinth, suggesting a place where honour has been fought for and held. The fulmars nesting on its craggy ledges further emphasise its aura of near-smug serenity. Seen from the mainland or the sea, its romantic profile on Beblowe Crag hints at a place as legendary as any Arthurian knight might have wished for. Reminiscent of St Michael's Mount in Cornwall and Mont Saint Michelle in Normandy, Lindisfarne Castle, too, functions as a visual lure which magnetises people and draws them off the road of humdrum, everyday lives.

Closer inspection, though, hints at a different reality: the building atop the rock is small for a castle; its roofs are finished with dark-orange pantiles. It is, in fact, an Edwardian villa in a bower of valerian atop a fifteen century fort. But the twentieth century adventurer need not be disappointed by the discovery that, far from being ancient, the castle is less than a hundred years old, for the amused genius behind this twentieth century contrivance got it exactly right.

The architect, Edward Lutyens, built on the 'daintie little forte' that already existed and endowed it with Tudor-revival features to delight the imagination: portcullis, buttresses, mullion windows, beamed ceilings, hammer-nail doors, and topped it all off with a tongue-in-cheek pantile roof.

It was in that charmed, leisured period at the beginning of the century (when summers were long and sunny and the privileged took proper long summer holidays which frequently included adventurous excursions in leather-upholstered motor cars equipped with wooden picnic hampers) that Edward Hudson, the inspired founder of *Country Life* magazine, first visited the Holy Island of Lindisfarne. Edward Hudson was accompanied by Peter Anderson Graham, editor of *Country Life* and author of *Highways and Byways in Northumbria*. They were scouting for suitable properties to include in the magazine and, although it would be some years before Lindisfarne Castle achieved that distinction, Hudson was immediately impressed by its potential. Finding the place unoccupied, the two warmed to adventure and laid siege to its interior by scaling the crags and walls.

It was, of course, precisely to sight invaders, particularly Scots invaders, and to stop them from scaling its walls, that the castle was originally built. In reality the castle was more of a fort and, according to a seventeenth century report, 'a daintie little fort' at that. In 1539, two years after the Dissolution of the Monasteries, The Crown ordered that all 'havens should be fenced with bulwarks and blockhouses against the Scots' and ten years later a fortification was built on Beblowe Crag from stone taken from the Priory. The Priory itself was converted into military storehouses and stables. In the meantime the 59th Benedictine prior of Lindisfarne had been pensioned off as Bishop of Berwick and Henry VIII was awarded the Priory.

The fortress lost its military importance after the accession of James VI to the English throne in 1603. In 1675 a garrison of almost thirty soldiers held the castle under a Captain Rugg who, in a rhyming letter to Charles I, signed himself: 'The great Commander of the Gormorants/The Geese and Ganders of these Hallowed Lands'.

Visitors at the time described 'a daintie little fort [in which] lives Captain Rugg who is as famous for his generous and free entertainment of strangers as for his great bottle nose, which is the largest I have ever seen. There are neat, warm and convenient rooms in this little fort'.

But the castle's last inhabitants before Hudson's 'siege' were coastguards who left behind the disorder and squalor associated with a place which has lost its true function. Far from putting Hudson off, the fort's dereliction encouraged him to believe that he might be able to make something quite remarkable of it.

Enchanted by the island's timeless tranquillity, and struck by the potential to turn the ruin of the fort on the crag into a holiday home with stunning sea-views and with an Arthur Ransome-like atmosphere of adventure, by January 1902 Hudson had negotiated the purchase of the castle from The Crown. His excitement must have been further inflamed by the contemporary passion among the literary circles he moved in for restoring and inhabiting ruined castles. He summoned the architect Lutyens to the site with a telegram: 'Have Got Lindisfarne'.

Almost the same age as Hudson, at 33 Edwin Lutyens was already the leading country house architect of his day. His reputation was built on his 'Surrey picturesque' period, but recent work revealed him to be eclectic and original with an unusual sympathy for texture and the use of local materials. His work at Lindisfarne did not disappoint. Lutyens created a series of strong, sparse interiors retaining exposed stone walls married here and there with white-wash. Today a wall of the barrel-vaulted Ship Room is painted a dark-olive green, and a wall of the Dining Room in stunning *lapis lazuli*.

The atmosphere of the interior derives from an intriguing blend of medieval and Dutch features, the latter particularly appropriate given the location of the castle on old east coast trading routes with the Low Countries. And the unpretentious, solid wooden furniture, set on herring-bone brick floors covered with old patterned carpets and decked with shining brassware and pottery, suggests a place to which travellers have returned from inspiring adventures.

Later Gertrude Jekyll came too, following in the footsteps of Lutyens, a pilgrimage repeated before in other house and garden collaborations of the duo whose names now have a legendary ring. Lindisfarne Castle, too, would have a garden. The redoubtable Miss Jekyll, who had introduced Lutyens to Hudson, wisely rejected her client's ambitious scheme for a water garden in a hollow north of the castle. She knew that a windswept, long-wintering northern landscape such as this would require a more down-to-earth approach and took seriously the hard-won solutions which had been grappled for down the centuries by Northumbrian horticulturists.

This garden would need high walls to protect all but the hardiest shrubs from leaf-burning sea winds and ravaging rabbits. Its plants would have to be carefully chosen to thrive in that sandy soil: sea thrift, rosemary, carnations, sea-holly, iris, poppies. To place a walled garden at some distance from the house was established Northumbrian tradition. Lutyens and Jekyll wanted it to be seen from the bird's-eye view of the main rooms in the castle, too. And so it was situated along the south-facing line of the dry stone dyke some five hundred yards from the castle.

The original 1911 plans for the garden came to light among other Jekyll papers at Berkeley University, California and are used as a ground plan by the National Trust which strives to maintain the garden in the spirit of its creator's intentions. And so today, within the enclosed wind-free haven, visitors (having borrowed the key to its gate at the castle) might sit to enjoy the results of Miss Jekyll's labours: sedum-covered paved paths, where clumps of sea thrift nestle in the cracks of paths lined with campion and rampant herbaceous borders scented with roses and lavender. In late spring it is not unlikely that a brooding duck might enjoy the sanctuary too, finding here a wind and fox-free zone in which to introduce her chicks to a gentler world than the coarse grassed dunelands beyond its walls.

Lindisfarne Castle, a property of the National Trust, and the harbour, attract most of the island's day trippers. If in winter there is still a sense of people and wildlife living together in simple balance, crowds during the rest of the year remind one of Lindisfarne's fragility. The management of visitors unceasingly challenges English Nature:

> *Even well-intentioned visitors can, simply by their interest, pose a threat to the wildlife. If birds are disturbed in the sanctuary areas during the shooting season by bait-digging, for example, they have nowhere else to go, and whole broods of birds may be lost if dogs run uncontrolled through the dunes during the nesting season.*

Most of the dunes are stable but may be damaged if too many people walking over them destroy the plant cover thereby allowing the wind to raise the loose sand and set it on the move again. Our main aims are to safeguard the wildfowl and wader populations and the sand dune systems.

This calls for control of activities like wildfowling, bait-digging and horse-riding, all done under licence or permit within less sensitive zones of the island. Camping and caravanning have never been allowed on the island. Campfires are a major threat, particularly in dry weather when dune grasses can be set alight by a single spark. English Nature itself has almost entirely sacrificed the use of off-road vehicles in the hope that its example will be taken seriously by the owners of four-wheel drive vehicles.

Fortunately, only an estimated ten per cent of visitors leave the village and harbour to walk on the reserve, and most of those who do keep to paths mindful of the fragility of the area.

The harbour sits centre-stage, a semi-circular haven for wheeling birds, fishing boats, pleasure craft, upturned boat sheds and a straggle of wooden fishermen's huts, wonky piles of lobster creels laced with vivid orange and turquoise netting, and wooden fishing boxes collected from places as far flung as Pittenweem and Eyemouth. The handsome herring houses where fish were once cured and smoked as industriously as lime was kilned, are now converted to comfortable homes with views of the harbour and the Castle.

Tourism and fishing are the island's remaining industries. It is greatly to the credit of the islanders that, as the fishing has dwindled, they have directed the course of tourism, always striving to strike the balance between the income they need to survive and the fragility of the island's ecology.

The sea, though, is the great protector of its unlikely gift, ensuring that incomers arrive when the tide is low, but go away again as it rises, leaving the place at peace with itself.

SIX

CONEY WARREN

North Shore to the Causeway

THE Snook guards its secrets well. It is a fragile dune-landscape, almost an island itself, a place apart, severed from Holy Island at high tide but for a narrow strip of sand and marram grass. The casual observer might conclude that there is nothing much here but dunes anyway.

The first New Year's day morning I spent on the island was bright and clear, the tide full-in to the bank by midday when gathering clouds were preceded by a rainbow arching from Snook to the Back Skeins. In the afternoon I disturbed curlews on the causewayside of Primrose Bank on the way to watch Brent geese grazing the luxuriant swads of *zostera* between the Wideopens and Sandsides.

Later, clusters of curlews elegantly flutter dark-winged against the sun. Sudden change of direction renders them silver, as-if-by-magic, and the village beyond becomes black and solid as *passe-partout*. This is one of thousands of visual island mantras I shall never forget.

The afternoon of New Year's Eve had been arrestingly dramatic. Walking on the Snook I noticed a man perched high on Primrose Bank, dark-sweatered, clutching a shotgun, immobile, with his head turned towards Snook Point. Watching, concealed, I wondered what would happen and could scarcely believe my eyes when a posse of maybe twenty men and older boys appeared, strung out in a line from Primrose Bank to the North Shore, each with a shotgun to the ready.

Passing Snook House garden, they saw me and their greeting dispelled my apprehension: they had seen four foxes but killed none. The foxes had to be flushed out and killed, they said, for they were plundering the refuse bins and attacking the village hens.

In winter you can feel the presence of foxes lurking unseen around Snook Point. Their white stools, encrusted with fur and bone of bird and rabbit, lie underfoot. The reserve warden had described how they scavenge the tide mark out on the North Shore beyond the Swinhoe Goat, scrawny and hungry. The image persisted, but it was several years before I saw their fleeting wraith-like forms diffuse through the sea's spume. The next mid-summer, from the crest of Jock Mathison's Bank, I watched two cubs enter the vast sea-stage of the North Shore towards sunset. They gambolled and teased each other, rolling and running, until they caught my scent and vanished like quicksilver, each in a different direction. The very first time I met Robin Henderson (we bumped into each other at the Post Office), he expressed surprise that I had never seen the breeding foxes before that, and even more surprise that I should particularly wish to do so.

* * *

On a wild, grey day the Snook seems God-forsaken. And when white mists drape round the Tower between warm and cool spells of weather, to swirl in spiralling shrouds through the sward, the sight of the Snook sends shivers up the spine. When, rarely, snow blankets it beneath a blue and almond-pink sky, or in spring when the dunes are jewel-bedecked with miniature violets and heady with the ecstatic song of wheatear and meadow lark, it announces itself as a modest earthly paradise.

When the summer sun shines the live-long day, its shadow expands and retracts in a circle round the battlemented gnomon of the Tower, transforming it into a giant sundial. The Tower was part of an eighteenth century coal boring operation and, more recently, almost certainly part of the salmon fishing industry as a lookout over the North Shore, its interior a stable for horses.

There is no reason for the throng to come here. The dedicated few who seek it out approach cautiously, on foot, respecting this protected habitat of wild things and the privacy of the residents at Snook House and the Tower. Members of botanical clubs can be seen in midsummer, kneeling as if in a mosque of Mecca, painstakingly examining the dune grasses which might answer their fervent wish to spot the rare coral orchid or dune helliborine. And in May and October, bird-watchers congregate in posses, pursuing exhausted and sometimes rare migrants which flutter onto this first landfall after arduous North Sea crossings. Oblivious to the fine focus of binoculars and telescopes, they build up strength to continue the journey, here in the garden of Snook House and in lanes and by-ways throughout the island: hoopoe, grey shrike, Pallas's warbler. Sightings of these birds, and more, are possible prizes.

Snook House was once a salmon fishing station, sister to the one which still operates away across the North Shore at Goswick. It was a thriving place until 1926 when Jack Hope's father, the last manager of the Snook fishing station, closed the door forever and moved his family, goods and gear, over to Goswick. Jack Hope, who still visits the island from time to time, was one of ten children raised at the Snook.

Jack remembers that the family lived in two rooms at the far end of the house. The rest was given over to seasonal salmon fishermen who came to the island in May and left in September. The itinerants entered their quarters by a separate door outwith the wall of the family garden. They mended their nets on the grass sward outside the bothy, or in the vast interior 'net room' which was also their refectory. They carried the glittering fish in boxes up an outside stair and laid them out, sorted and ready, to be uplifted by the waggon-carts which transported the catch to the mainland – over the sands to Goswick. They came from as far away as Montrose. See, here is a stone ale bottle stamped with the name of the Scottish town, in perfect condition, unearthed from the sand.

But the community here was never regarded as 'Holy Island'. And still today villagers will say, 'Oh, so you're from the Snook'. Jack Hope remembers his small child self, hiding in the kitchen cupboard of Snook House when 'Holy Islanders' came to visit his parents, peeping out at a row of long skirts and black-heeled shoes, accompanied by handbags lined up under the wooden settle by the vast fireplace.

He returns to reminisce on the bench outside the garden wall, to look for lark's nests and shelduck and the flowers which form part of his earliest memories. He notices the unwelcome recent addition to the area's flora which English Nature is concerned about: pirri-pirri burr, a plant from the southern hemisphere which is infesting the flower-rich dune slacks. It found its way to the island via the Tweed valley, where it arrived in the fleece of New Zealand sheep. It clings to clothing and to the hair of visiting dogs and indigenous animals and mats the feathers of birds.

Summer days. Bygone days. Today, like age-old June days, a rich variety of flowers including early and northern marsh-orchids flourishes on Lindisfarne and on the Snook.

The great Scottish architect, Charles Rennie Mackintosh, spent his honeymoon on the island in 1900, returning in 1901, a year which marked a transition in his creative life and resulted in the poetic expression contained in a manuscript of the period:

> *Art is the flower – Life is the green leaf. Let every artist strive to make his flower a beautiful living thing – something that will convince the world that there may be – there are – things more precious – more beautiful – more lasting than life.*

Nature, and wild flowers in particular, inspired Mackintosh's furniture and the decorative details of his architecture. Petals, seedpods, flower stems and tendrils were all part of the design vocabulary he amassed as pencil sketches ever since his student days. But under the timeless tranquillity of Lindisfarne's influence, he began to produce exquisite, mature watercolours inspired by individual flowers: Sea Pink, Bugloss, Pimpernel, Yellow Clover, Purple Mallows, Milk Thistle, Mustard-seed Flower, Storksbill, Cranesbill, Brook Weed and Hound's Tongue.

In the same manuscript he wrote:

> *... you must offer real, living, beautifully coloured flowers – flowers that grow from but above the green leaf – flowers that are not dead – are not dying – not artificial – real flowers – you must offer the flowers of the art that is in you – the symbols of all that is noble – and beautiful – and inspiring – flowers that will often change a colourless leaf – into an estimated thoughtful thing.*

The art historian, Roger Billcliffe, who

has studied Charles Rennie Mackintosh's watercolours closely, observes that his marriage to Margaret Macdonald was probably the catalyst which inspired the evolution of the flower drawings into pictures in their own right and not simply sketches as ideas in his pattern-book of decorative details:

> *As a bachelor, Mackintosh made whistle-stop tours around the countryside, filling his books with dozens of sketches. As a married man, his annual holiday was more often spent in one place with Margaret, and occasionally with Herbert and Frances MacNair. With more time available to him, the drawings became increasingly pictorial, and the colour washes on the flowers were probably added in the seclusion of their cottage or hotel room.*
>
> *At the time, Mackintosh also began to sign and elaborately inscribe his drawings, often including his wife's initials, a practice which has led to suggestions that the colour washes on his drawings were added by Margaret. However, as nobody was allowed to touch Mackintosh's work, not even his wife, the initials simply indicate – in what was by then practically a family album – the people who were with him when he made the drawing. Hence the appearance of Herbert and Frances MacNair's initials, and those of Charles Macdonald, in some of the Holy Island sketches of 1901.*

The assistant English Nature warden pauses at the back door of Snook House on his weekly 'butterfly walk', pleased that the nettles there, which support the eggs of the

only colony of blue butterflies on the island,
have been allowed to thrive. The butterfly
hibernates in the roof spaces of the house over
winter and lays eggs again in the spring.

In a dune hollow behind the house, fanned
by gentle sea breezes, the six-spot burnet
mates and pupates. A carpet of bird's foot
trefoil conceals masses of the black and pink
moths, recently emerged from black chrysalis
skins on paper-like sacks glued to marram
grass stalks. Soon the burnets will discover
the enjoyment of blue-and-purple-pink viper's
bugloss, here and elsewhere on the island.
Later the hairy caterpillar of the cinnabar
moth will consume the flowers and leaves of
the massed ragwort upon which its life
depends.

Occasionally, on a mystical Yeatsian-night
when moths come flickering out with the
stars, one of the wardens will leave a box
fitted with a blue-neon light in the garden
overnight. Attracted moths enter the box and
land in its soft interior lining. Some of the
catch will be sent to be examined by lepidop-
terists in Durham. In June 1986 came the
first identification of the dog's tooth moth in
Northumberland for exactly a century; and,
later that month, a bountiful night produced
a splendid poplar hawk, several caddis, a
garden carpet, colons, shears and brightlines
and many hebrew character moths.

Throughout Britain today rabbits have
reached plague proportions. Like the island,
the Snook is overrun with the menace which
not even the breeding foxes on Primrose
Bank can curb. But the Snook was once one

of the most valued stretches of land on the north-east coast, precisely because of rabbits. Indeed, a fifteenth century map of *Insula Sacra Lindisfarensis* by Speed records the Snook as Conney Warren. The map identifies a strange T-shaped marking at the entrance to the Snook which may be a sentry post, or even a gibbet, since in those days rabbit warrens were jealously guarded to provide meat for the tables of the Bishop of Durham and the wealthy of the north.

Back in 1984 Newcastle University made an extensive study of rabbits at the north end of the Snook. At that time hundreds of rabbit holes were given tiny wooden number plates, Beatrix Potter-style, which corresponded to markings on the animals themselves. And they were observed from a high-stilted green hide, day and night, by dedicated researchers. They gathered enough information to refute some of the findings of a 1960s survey elsewhere upon which the book *Watership Down* was based.

> *Someone else should write a novel showing that rabbits behave not quite like that. Rabbits are solitary creatures although the females keep together in a loose sort of way, while the males avoid each other and if they meet directly, they fight. A female has an average of three litters in the summer months and can be lactating for a new brood before the one before has weaned. So rabbits have to start fending for themselves at around four weeks old.*

English Nature does become concerned

when the rabbit population gets out of hand, but insists that the island's ecology needs them. Rabbits graze the dune slacks and help to curb the encroachment of rank grasses, scrub and creeping willow which gradually oust the orchids. If the rabbits did not graze the dunes, other means of doing so would have to be considered. Indeed, at the northern end of the island, a number of exotic sheep including Hebrideans and Soay are busy reducing the grass.

*   *   *

The trek beyond Snook Point, across the Sand Ridge to Goswick, is not for the faint-hearted or inexperienced. Local knowledge of this vast sea domain is required to deliver the traveller safely through patches of quicksand, unexploded World War II mines and effusive tides.

There are wrecks here too, their broken wooden ribs or barnacled, rusting hulls more or less visible through the shifting sand, so aged that no one remembers the circumstances of their grounding. Once the island had two lifeboat stations: the one in the village and one beyond Snook House which was closed in the 1930s. Ralph Wilson, for many years harbourmaster and one of Holy Island's older inhabitants (born and bred), is full of stories which he is in the process of recording. One of these concerns the Snook Lifeboat. Ralph Wilson would tell you the story much better than I. Hopefully, one day, he will write his own island book:

We always knew which was which by the blast on the horn. Two blasts for the Holy Island and three for the Snook lifeboat. One day me and my friend (we were about ten years old at the time; he's buried in the kirkyard now) were sitting in the schoolroom (boring; it was very boring) when three blasts went off.

We children kept looking down (we had to pretend nothing was happening; daft to think of doing that to children; near killed our sense of wonder); but we also managed to look at each other sideways in amazement: 'The Snook lifeboat!' Rescues didn't happen often at the Snook. Soon we could hear the heavy boots of the men belting through the square to get out the cart-horses from the field. You could hear a pin drop in the classroom as we pretended to practise our handwriting, but really our thoughts were out of that schoolroom window altogether.

In ten minutes they all rushed past the window again, running like their lives depended on it with the horses clattering for all they were worth, out on the road to the Snook. Mercifully the playground bell rang and without saying a word to each other or anyone else, we were running like the wind, not on the road, you understand, but over the dunes. My father was among the men and he'd have thrashed us sound if he'd caught us playing truant.

It was quite a sight to see all the men, twenty or so, dressed in dark clothes and waders, just like I am now. I can see it as if it were yesterday. You'll have seen pictures of the old lifeboats, so you'll know what huge things they were that the men had to pull out, even though they were on metal wheels. Once out of the shed and down on the sands, the boat on wheels was pulled out to sea by the horses with the men on board.

We boys didn't know what was up as we hid in the dune grass. The mist was down thick, you see. But we waited for our moment and when the men and horses took off with the lifeboat we raced cunningly behind, like little foxes, finally leaping on to the back of the boat where we held on for dear life. We were carried like this for maybe half a mile through the fog over the North Shore sands until we reached the water which was the cue for us to get down fast. Peering round aft we saw a great sailing vessel looking out of the fog. Not being in the water made it look bigger than any boat I'd ever seen. I near burst with laughing at the sight of it marooned there in inches of water where the tide had left it high and dry.

Father and the others splashed out to it and climbed up the rope ladders suspended from its side. They wanted to help, of course, and to give advice since they knew the lie of the land better than anyone. Then we heard a voice booming out through the fog (scary? it was scary, I tell you): 'the first man to climb to the top will have his fingers cut off.' And as the fog slowly lifted there he was, the Norwegian captain on the deck, telescope in hand; he had the most enormous, thick white whiskers I ever saw. But that's where we boys had to be off ....! fast. Later we heard the fishermen discussing how the ship was carrying contraband goods and the captain would rather sit out the tide to be refloated than allow any British aboard.

Beyond the Goat are the drift nets, cobles and tractors of the Goswick salmon fishing station. Paradoxically, since it is situated in England, the Goswick station is the most southerly Scottish salmon fishing station.

From the Tweed to the Humber, over many centuries, fishermen have hauled into shore in cobles – flat bottomed, open craft, clinker-built of overlapping planks clinched with copper nails, their design dating back to the Vikings and unique to this part of the coast-line. Cobles are large enough to bring in a decent catch, but small enough to be owned by an individual who can, as the Goswick fishers do, live out the fishing season in a beached caravan.

Somewhere on the Sand Ridge towards Goswick, the thick, ridged wheels of a buried tractor emerge eerily through the sand. Did it overturn and was it claimed by the tide? Did it hit a patch of quicksand? Whatever its fate was, it must have been a loss to the Goswick fishermen who depend on tractors to meet the coble at the shoreline and haul it in.

Long before Snook and Goswick became fishing stations, St Cuthbert and the monks of Holy Island were granted rights to the fish caught at Hallowstell in the mouth of the Tweed. Tweed Salmon has been exported to London and elsewhere since at least the thirteenth century in pickled or salted form and more recently on ice.

My eyes trace the featureless sands and the mainland. Once I walked over to Goswick where, except in minor details, the old fishing station is architecturally identical to the former

Snook station. On the mainland between Goswick and Snook Point, an old ice-house, built cavern-like into the dunes, received the glittering daily salmon catch from Holy Island. That was before the tides changed and the Snook fishing ceased forever.

Looking back towards Lindisfarne, beyond the dunes of Snook Point, cars and vans ply the umbilical causeway like Dinky toys. It amuses me to see the symbols of the world to which I must return from this distant perspective. Meanwhile I absorb the untellable experience of vast waters and sky and the fabulous sand space between, riveted with glittering waters which attract crowds of wader birds to feed at their margins.

Here dive-bombing terns screech in season, red-throated in defence of their territory. The feathers of seabirds roll in the wind like tumbleweed, and the occasional mermaid's purse, double-sunrise or razorshell appears like irresistible treasure. Cormorants muse and dry their wings on the shoreline near the point where the North Goat swirls in and recedes twice every 24 hours to meet the South Low and encircle the island.

SEVEN

TO
THE FARNES

*A Boat Trip
from Seahouses*

THERE are Glad Tidings everywhere
you look in Seahouses Harbour:
Glad Tidings I, II, III, and IV.
MFVs – Motorised Fishing Vessels – all the
property of Billy Shiels who, alongside several
other weatherbeaten fishermen-turned-
entrepreneurs, deals in trips to the Farne
Islands. The Farnes are one of the most
important nature reserves in the British Isles
and over 250 species of birds recorded there
are completely protected. Visitors may land
on the Inner Farne and Staple Island from
April to September, with restricted access
during the breeding season.

As we wait to embark on Glad Tidings II,
I reflect that Seahouses lost its old stone heart
to a concrete and brick jungle long ago. The
world and his wife is here these days and most
take a trip to the Farnes between sampling
'the best fish and chips in the north east' and
exploring emporia offering imported sea
shells, lettered rock, silly hats and plastic
knick-knack souvenirs to the rhythmic chant

emanating from Johnny's Prize Bingo.

As we queue with the crowd, Cuthbert, who left Lindisfarne for the Farnes when it became 'too cosmopolitan', springs uneasily to mind. If he were alive today, these islands would not be far enough away from all this bustle. However, we are happy enough to pull out of the harbour at last, in one of the boats in a flotilla of MFVs – to follow in his footsteps, to see the site of his sanctuary, to explore the National Trust's wooden walkway on Inner Farne among nesting birds.

A grey spring sea teases the boat and playfully washes its waters over the seated passengers who take refuge under waterproofs and woollen hats. But they stand up almost reverentially when the group of islands that make up the Farnes become close enough to be distinctive: Inner Farne, Staple Island, Brownsman North and South Wamses and Longstone.

In fact there are thirty islands here, some exposed only at low water, with extraordinary names like Fang, Glororum Shad and Elbow. Like parts of the Holy Island of Lindisfarne, the Farnes mark the eastern end of the Great Whin Sill. They share with Holy Island, too, a sense of mystique: the double sanctity of nature reserve and Holy place. And the Farnes have their legends too. A heroine, this time: Grace Darling, Victorian superstar, who assisted her father in the rescue of sailors from the jaws of the rapacious sea.

But it is fair to say that the Farne Islands cannot match all of Lindisfarne's cachets. You cannot book lodgings here and retreat from the so-called civilized world; you must return after an hour with Billy Shiels' MFV or one of the other company-owned boats. You cannot wander for hours, exploring coves and beaches. You cannot easily play the pilgrim as one of a party of thirty or one hundred sheepishly treading the National Trust boardwalks on Inner Farne.

The boatman quietens the engine and one of the first things he says is that, in recent years, divers with their boats and gear have scared off large numbers of the seals. He adds reassuringly that he should be able to find some for us. This is, after all, the head-quarters of one of the largest British colonies of the grey seal. Sure enough. Minutes later a colony of dark bull seals, mottled cows and last year's pups comes into view, perched precariously on the promontory of Stamford Haven at the entrance to Cuthbert's Cove.

The swarthy skipper knows nearly everything about the seals. He tells us that most of the births take place in November after almost a year of gestation; that each cow produces a single pup; that her milk is very rich; that a well-fed pup can treble its birth weight after 18 days when it is weaned. For another week or so the pups stay in the rockbound nurseries, living on the fat they amassed so quickly, before taking to sea where they must fend for themselves. Newborn pups are covered with white hair, long and soft, which is replaced by a shorter, greyish coat at four weeks old. Many will find their way over to Lindisfarne where they assemble in Coves Haven and sing on the rocks during summer low tides.

The song of the seals has been heard in these parts for more than eight centuries. Throughout this time they were slaughtered for blubber and skins, so that at the beginning of this century only a hundred or so animals remained. Twentieth century protection of the seals brought new problems. The seal population soared to nine thousand in the 1970s and, in competition for limited space on the reserve, many of the adults had become aggressive, their pups unhealthily afflicted with septic eyes and wounds. Almost one quarter of the pups starved to death: in particularly crowded spaces the death rate doubled.

Brownsman and Staple Island, the main nurseries, were devastated as plants and topsoil virtually disappeared at the end of the breeding season. Throughout the islands, ground nesting birds were displaced by the seal population boom. Now the number of seal births and their location is carefully controlled without actually culling the seals. Locals on the mainland report that they can hear the distant cry of new-born seals waiting to be suckled out here on these rocks in winter, when the wind is in the right direction.

Inner Farne, the largest of the islands, is wedge-shaped with a rock stack at its southern end. A National Trust ranger takes tickets as the passengers land to meander slowly up past the chapel, the exhibition centre, the remarkably unbothered birds nesting by the boardwalk, and on as far as they can go to the edge of the whin stack.

It is extraordinary to stand here, above the

breeding ledges, with the toes of your boots touching the highest nests: the kittiwakes' cup-shaped nests which are literally glued onto any suitable cranny. Looking down, the grey rock is whitewashed with thick streaks of guano, its ledges supporting layer upon layer of billing, cooing, calling, diving, wheeling, feeding, nesting seabirds. Ledge after ledge descending sheer to the sea: nesting couples of grand, oriental-looking shags side-by-side with mating kittiwakes, screeching to fend off third parties. And the sky beyond the stack is filled with the almost frenzied flight of hundreds of birds coming-and-going to supply nesting mates to ensure the survival of the species.

Kittiwakes, shag, guillemot, fulmar and razorbill make their home on the cliffs of Inner Farne. There is a puffin colony too, and hundreds of terns – Arctic, common, roseate and sandwich – which nest in St Cuthbert's Cove and on the island's topsoil. Mallard and shelduck breed in relatively small numbers, but mallard, widgeon and scoter sometimes arrive in unexpectedly large flocks. In May and June over a thousand eiders nest in congregations on scrapes in the ground.

Cormorants and shags breed here, and are also present throughout the year. In winter hundreds of shags move down from Scottish colonies like the Bass Rock and the Isle of May, while many birds of the Farne population move south. Eight species of petrel have been recorded, but only the fulmar breeds on the islands and parties of Manx shearwater arrive regularly in summer.

Before boarding Glad Tidings again, there is time to explore the fourteenth century chapel dedicated to St Cuthbert who died here in 687. Apart from this chapel and the chapel of St Mary (now the National Trust information centre), Prior Castell's tower and the monks' *hospitium,* all the other buildings on the islands were, or are, lighthouses.

It seems that Cuthbert was the first human to dwell on the Farnes because the presence of phantoms or demons who lived there frightened lesser mortals off. According to one source the ghouls were banished by Cuthbert to the islands west of Inner Farne. But they were still in evidence in the thirteenth century when a monk's description had them 'clad in cowls and riding upon goats, black in complexion, short in stature, their countenances most hideous, their heads long, the appearance of the whole troop horrible'.

Inner Farne boasts most of the islands' 125 recorded plants, a litany similar to Lindisfarne's: sea-thrift, silverweed, bugloss, ragwort, hemlock and many grasses. A species of borage which came originally from California grows round the buildings, but the characteristic plant is white campion which carpets the Farnes in summer.

The boat chugs on past the famous whin sill pinnacles off Staple Islands, an ornothologists' and photographers' paradise from May to late July, providing close-up views of nearly all the Farne's birds. Sometimes a few pairs of Arctic terns nest on the rocky beach.

Away to the north east is Longstone, whose 1826 lighthouse was once the home of Grace

Darling. In September 1838 she and her father set out to rescue eleven survivors of the 'SS Forfarshire' which went aground on Big Harcar.

As the boat heads back to Seahouses the noise of the engine eventually drowns out the cry of the birds, and I am struck by the sense that Lindisfarne and the Farnes are indeed powerfully linked, through the wildlife common to both places and through the monastic remains. The Farne Islands, too, are a gift from the sea.

ICARUS ON
LINDISFARNE

Icarus lies distressed –
A hapless piece of metal on the North Shore –
Victim of some mythological prank,
Alchemical salvage off a ship's prow,
      rivet holes agape.
Strolling islanders stop and say:
'A hopeless rusty thing
of no real use to anyone';
Give it a kick and turn away.
Not I – I strike a sounding here:
      on the birdlike form,
Shape suggesting fallen angels,
      shattered dreams,
and stay to burnish-up the wings.

BIBLIOGRAPHY

Backhouse, Janet: *The Lindisfarne Gospels*
(Oxford: Phaidon Press, 1981).

Bamford, C and W P Marsh: *Celtic
Christianity* (Inner Traditions/Lindisfarne
Press, 1987).

Billcliffe, Roger: *Mackintosh Watercolours:*
(John Murray Ltd, 1979).

Cartright, R A and D B: *The Holy Island of
Lindisfarne and the Farne Islands* (London:
David & Charles, 1976).

Lindisfarne Excavation Project Pamphlet:
Archeology on Lindisfarne (Department of
Archeology, University of Leicester,
1988).

Magnusson, Magnus: *Lindisfarne: The Cradle
Island* (Oriel Press, 1984).

The National Trust: *Lindisfarne Castle*
(1988).

Patterson, Andrew R M: *A Celtic Saga*
(Edinburgh: Saint Andrew Press, 1991).

Perry, Richard: *A Naturalist on Lindisfarne*
(Lindsay Drummond Ltd, 1946).

Thompson, William Irwin: *Passages About
Earth* (Massachusetts, USA: The
Lindisfarne Press, 1987).

The map which appears on the endpapers of this book has
been adapted from a fold-out map in the Richard Perry book,
A Naturalist on Lindisfarne (Lindsay Drummond Ltd, 1946).

South Low

Beal Point

Pales

Pales

Beal Shore

Point

The Low

The

Refuge Bcl

Beal
Sands

Sand

The Buys

Mud

50

Black Low

Ordnary Point

Mud

Fenhom Pt

Fenhom Mill

Common Slab

Scale

¼   ½   ¾   1 mile

The Snook

Tower
(Coal boring)

North S?

Shell hood

Big Bank

Widecpens

Poles

Primrose Bank

rims Way

Poles

Refuge
Box

Ford

Sh

The Swad

Poles

The Slakes

Sand

Mill Burn

enham Flats

Mud

The Blacks

Lowmoor
Point